The Pocket Dream

A comedy

Elly Brewer and Sandi Toksvig

Samuel French — London
New York - Toronto - Hollywood

Please see page xi for further copyright information

THE POCKET DREAM

First performed at the Nottingham Playhouse on 25th April 1991 with the following cast of characters:

Simon Beaumont **Theseus** **Mustardseed** **Quince** **Prologue**	Phelim McDermott
Phyllida Brewster **Hippolyta** **Helena** **Titania** **Starveling** **Moonshine**	Louisa Rix
Jo Payne **Hermia** **Puck** **Snout** **Wall**	Sandi Toksvig
Dave Hershaw **Philostrate** **Lysander** **Bottom** **Pyramus**	Neil Mullarkey
Felix Barker **Egeus** **Oberon** **Snug** **Lion**	Mac McDonald
Tom Brindle **Demetrius** **Peaseblossom** **Flute** **Thisbe**	Lee Simpson

Fairies: Blue Team, Red Team, Yellow Team

Directed by Pip Broughton
Designed by Jacqueline Gunn

It returned to the Nottingham Playhouse on 1st February 1992 and was subsequently presented by the Theatre of Comedy Company in association with the Nottingham Playhouse at the Albery Theatre, London, on 27th February 1992 with the following cast of characters:

Simon Beaumont **Theseus** **Mustardseed** **Quince** **Prologue**	Phelim McDermott
Phyllida Brewster **Hippolyta** **Helena** **Titania** **Starveling** **Moonshine**	Louisa Rix
Jo Payne **Hermia** **Puck** **Snout** **Wall**	Sandi Toksvig
Dave Hershaw **Philostrate** **Lysander** **Bottom** **Pyramus**	Clive Mantle
Felix Barker **Egeus** **Oberon** **Snug** **Lion**	Mike McShane
Tom Brindle **Demetrius** **Peaseblossom** **Flute** **Thisbe**	Lee Simpson

Fairies: Blue Team, Red Team, Yellow Team

Directed by Pip Broughton
Designed by Jacqueline Gunn

THE CHARACTERS

FELIX BARKER : Front of House Manager — a dapper man, with a gambling habit, who started at the theatre as a temporary barman and has climbed through the ranks by virtue of never having left. Ten years ago he was only passing through town after a spot of bother with an unpaid debt. He is not particularly interested in theatre and although used to dealing with the public, he is shy when it comes to anything related to being on stage.

JO PAYNE : Stage Manager — a fairly efficient worker with a no-nonsense attitude which manifests itself in flippancy. A small woman, she pays no attention to her personal appearance and wears unflattering glasses and theatre "blacks". Slightly contemptuous of Phyllida and her television work, Jo loves theatre, but has no desire to be an actress and has learnt her understudy parts with casual indifference, never expecting to go on.

PHYLLIDA BREWSTER : Actress — hired to play Hippolyta and Titania, Phyllida is not the most popular member of the cast, misguidedly believing she has the best interests of the show at heart as she constantly "advises" her fellow artistes on how to improve their performances. Trained at RADA, she is still bitter over not winning the gold acting medal. Phyllida's many close calls with stardom never led to the fame she so desperately seeks. Just turned 40, Phyllida's anxiety about her future has manifested itself in her choice of a young, virile, live-in-lover, which both pleases and worries her.

DAVE HERSHAW : Handyman/stage hand — an ex-fireman who was asked to leave as his constant mishaps were endangering his fellow crew. First introduced to the theatre as overnight fireman, Dave joined the staff full time shortly after his fire station burned down. This is Dave's first production and he's so thrilled with his new job that he's even learned the lines. His constant desire to help can be irritating, but it is difficult to get annoyed with him as he means so well and is unfailingly cheerful and optimistic.

TOM BRINDLE : Phyllida's boyfriend — a PE teacher at an all girls school in London who met Phyllida when she presented the drama prizes at speech day. They have been together for eighteen months — Tom is proud of her, truly loves her and insists that his other "excursions" mean nothing to him. Although not overly bright, Tom knows how to use his good looks to the best effect and has limitless confidence. He has come to get Phyllida back, after she walked out over a "misunderstanding" concerning a fellow member of staff (female). Tom knows the lines from The Dream as he spent many hours helping Phyllida learn hers.

SIMON BEAUMONT : Actor — extremely professional, with a long history in TIE, Simon has never made a name for himself in anything, although he is known as a "solid company member". His career includes several seasons in Regent's Park, one line in *Howard's Way* and several years in the touring version of *Privates on Parade*. Although he appears weedy, Simon's body is a temple for his work — he spends many hours honing his skills and is always first into the theatre to prepare for the show.

AUTHORS' NOTES

The Pocket Dream is set in a small theatre where the Henry Irving Strolling Players (HISP) Memorial Theatre are due to appear as part of a countrywide tour, to present *A Midsommer Night's Dreame*.

To reinforce the set-up, **Felix Barker** stood in the foyer before the play began, overseeing the smooth running of his Front of House area and **Tom Brindle** arrived as a member of the audience, had a proper ticket for the play and took his seat along with everyone else. Only **Jo, Dave** and **Tom** were ever seen effecting scene changes.

The original production employed Kirby's Flying Ballets who enabled Puck to fly, but where there is no access to a flying rig, then a similar effect might be achieved with Puck on roller skates or a skateboard, adapting the lines accordingly.

For the original staging of the play, a programme was produced in two halves— one for the "supposed" HISP play, complete with fake cast list and biographies for **Phyllida Brewster** and her leading man, the other with the genuine cast list and biographies.

The fake cast list and some background information on HISP are included in the following pages for use, if required, in promotional literature.

The Henry Irving Strolling Players Memorial Theatre

A bit of background...

One afternoon in 1975, a group of eager young theatricals chanced upon and much enjoyed a production which recreated the staging of Samuel Phelps's Sadler's Wells version of *A Midsommer Night's Dreame* from 1853. So much so, that we raced back to our digs in Balham and sat around the one electric bar to read the play aloud, each taking the role we coveted most.

Such was our enjoyment of this first spontaneous encounter with The Bard, that we were moved to consider how enriched our lives would be, were we to devote ourselves to The Great Man's work. Thus was The Henry Irving Strolling Players Memorial Theatre founded and from that moment on, we came to look upon *The Dreame* as our talisman.

HISP's founding philosophy is to present the pure and unadulterated works of The Bard, as close to their original form as the distance of years allows, and to illuminate them for the masses.

With all our productions, before a single iambic pentameter is vocalised, there are painstaking months of research into original pronunciations and stage directions. The company work by piecing together our performances, like theatrical detectives seeking every hidden subtlety and cunning nuance in the original text. And though some may think it radical, we sculpt our plays collaboratively, each actor helping out his fellow. What function a director, when The Bard is master and perfection is the single common goal?

Early appearances ranged from such diverse locations as the social club of United Biscuits (*As You Like It*), to the stage of the Open Air Theatre, Basildon (*Hamlet*). Then, having found our thespic feet, we progressed to school tours (*Romeo and Juliet*) and various incarceration units for the socially disadvantaged (*King Lear*). This phase of our development culminated in our most prestigious accolade to date: the Golden Chalks Award for "Best Shakespearean Tragedy in a Schools Touring Production, Northumbrian Region".

It was this award which lent credence to our quest to seek approval from a wider theatre-going public. Months of intense rehearsal gave birth to the Corps' most ambitious project to date: *A Midsommer Night's Dreame*.

A MIDSOMMER NIGHT'S DREAME
BY WILLIAM SHAKESPEARE

DRAMATIS PERSONAE

Theseus, Duke of Athens ....GRAHAM STUART
Hippolyta, Queen of the Amazons ....PHYLLIDA BREWSTER
Hermia, Egeus's Daughter, in love with Lysander ....THEADORA BENNET
Lysander, loved by Hermia ....ANTHONY HARPUR
Demetrius, suitor of Hermia ....PATRICK WARD
Helena, in love with Demetrius ....DEIRDRE DAVIES
Egeus, Hermia's Father ....PETER STEWART
Philostrate, Theseus' Master of the Revels ....MICHAEL PERRIN
Oberon, King of the Fairies ....CHRISTOPHER PACK
Titania, Queen of the Fairies ....PHYLLIDA BREWSTER
Puck, or Robin Goodfellow ....PAUL CHEDLOW

Fairies

Peaseblossom ....MARY BELL
Cobweb ....SIMON BEAUMONT
Moth ....ROBERT MACGREGOR
Mustardseed..MAX MACKENZIE

Peter Quince, a carpenter; Prologue ....MARY BELL
Nick Bottom, a weaver; Pyramus ....ADRIAN MICHAELS
Francis Flute. a bellows-mender; Thisbe ....RICHARD THISTLE
Tom Snout, a tinker; Wall...JOHN HENDERSON
Snug, a joiner; Lion ....MARK LEVY
Robin Starveling, a tailor; Moonshine ....WASYL NIMENKO

Fairies attending on Oberon and Titania

Katie Bradford	Jared Baker	Noella Bello
Vanessa Campbell	Billy Clark	Steven Brandy
Rickie Downey	Elaine Francisco	Elizabeth Faulds
Jack Falconer	Lorraine Francisco	Anna Hilton
Dominic Gilmore	Zoë John	Jess Hilton
Aaron Gourlay	Damian Irish	Rachel Mamauag
Jodi Neill	Amiir Saleem	Jay aul Murphy
Salah Eddine Salik	Nicholas Tapp	Piers Robinson
Emily Thomas	Chloe Ward	Mario Roberto Salvato
Mary Thomas	Cassandra Zenthner	Tyrone Ward

Understudies: Carly Cheeseman, Logan Coutts, Laura McGrath, Sebastian Zito

Lords and Attendants to Theseus and Hippolyta
(with thanks to those members of the cast who volunteered their spouses!)

ACT I

House Lights to half

JO (*voice over*) Ladies and Gentlemen...

Pause while the audience settle

...at this performance by the Henry Irving Strolling Players of *A Midsommer Night's Dreame*, the part of Theseus will be played by Simon Beaumont. May I remind you, Ladies and Gentlemen, that the taking of photographs and the use of tape recorders is prohibited. Thank you.

House Lights out

As the CURTAIN *rises, Mendelssohn's "Dream" music is heard. Smoke drifts across the stage. A small band of Fairies dance up through the audience and on to the stage. As they dance we notice some are slightly oddball — one has heavy boots on, one a broken leg, one trainers etc. In the distance a clock strikes and the Fairies disappear*

A flat showing an entrance to the Duke's palace flies in as Theseus (Simon) and Hippolyta (Phyllida) enter UL *and pose regally in front of the flat*

THESEUS (SIMON)
    Now, fair Hippolyta, our nuptial hour
    Draws on apace. Four happy days bring in
    Another moon — but O, methinks how slow
    This old moon wanes! She lingers my desires,
    Like to a stepdame or a dowager
    Long withering out a young man's revenue.

HIPPOLYTA (PHYLLIDA)
>Four days will quickly steep themselves in night;
>Four nights will quickly dream away the time:
>And then the moon — like to a silver bow
>New-bent in heaven — shall behold the night
>Of our solemnities.

THESEUS (SIMON) *(gesturing* L *with confidence)*
>Go, Philostrate,
>Stir up the Athenian youth to merriments,
>Awake the pert and nimble spirit of...

(It dawns on him that no-one has followed him on stage)

*Phyllida smiles gamely at Simon and the audience, confident that she has
no more speeches and it can't be her who has gone wrong. After a pause,
Simon soldiers on, turning to the other side in case Philostrate has entered*
R *by mistake*

>Go, Philostrate...

*Pause. We hear Jo and Dave running backstage calling to each other, as
doors slam*

PHYLLIDA *(stage whisper)* Where the hell is he?

SIMON *(out of the side of his mouth)* I don't know. *(He takes Phyllida
firmly by the arm and moves her* DR*)*

PHYLLIDA What are you doing?

SIMON Just act royal. *(Brightly)* Come, my lady. Uh ... let us hither ...
(moving Phyllida L *to the prompt corner)* ... and go ... thither.

HIPPOLYTA (PHYLLIDA) *(rallying round))*
>And I shall play me on my ... zither.

SIMON *(looking desperately for help))* Jo? Jo?

JO *(off)* What?

SIMON Where is everybody?

JO *(off)* I don't know. I can't find anyone. Go round one more time.

SIMON OK.

Dragging Phyllida, the two return to their original positions

THESEUS (SIMON) *(a little faster)*
>Now, fair Hippolyta, our nuptial hour

> Draws on apace. Four happy days bring in
> Another moon — but O, methinks how...
> *(looking to the L wings)... slow*
> This old moon wanes! She lingers my desires,
> Like to a stepdame or a dowager
> Long withering out a young man's revenue.

HIPPOLYTA (PHYLLIDA)

> Four days will quickly steep themselves in night;
> Four nights will quickly dream away the time——

THESEUS (SIMON) *(interrupting)*

> > Go, Philostrate...

The flat behind them drops, making a terrible noise. Phyllida and Simon react

PHYLLIDA Oh for God's sake. That's it. *(Looking to the prompt corner)* Where the hell's the Company Manager? I'm waiting. Where is he?

JO *(off)* Er...Wandsworth Prison. *(Or local reference)*

PHYLLIDA Yes, well get him. I... what?

Jo, the Stage Manager, wearing cans and carrying the prompt book, beckons to Phyllida from the prompt corner

No. You come here.

JO *(slowly creeping on stage, avoiding looking at the audience)* Apparently...er...some misunderstanding with one of the fairies last night. I must say I thought she looked older... anyway, they've refused bail. *(Turning to exit, she sees the audience for the first time and pales)* Oh my God!

Jo exits

PHYLLIDA How distasteful. Wardrobe, this neckline still isn't laying right...Of course "now", Betty.

Phyllida exits R

(Muttering as she goes) I'm sure you'll recollect I mentioned it twice in the fitting.

Simon is appalled to find himself alone, c. *Still attempting to maintain his poise as Theseus, he scurries to the prompt corner and drags Jo on. Jo is on the phone and the cord to the receiver stretches with her to* c

JO *(on the phone)* I must speak to Mr Barker. ... Well where is he?
SIMON *(to Jo)* If the Company Manager's not here you'd better say something.

Jo turns to speak to the audience, realizes she is still on the phone and lets it go — it flies off into the prompt corner

Phyllida appears R

Simon goes to stand next to Phyllida

JO *(clearing her throat, speaking very quietly, nervous)* Ladies and gentlemen ... so sorry ... one or two tiny problems with the ...
VOICE (TOM) FROM AUDIENCE Speak up!

Simon, Phyllida and Jo all try to see who has shouted

JO *(too loud)* Ladies and gentlemen, we do seem to have one or two gremlins in the works this evening. *(Loud, nervous laugh. To the flies)* Alex, could you take the flat out, please.

The flat flies out

Everything's now under control and er...

As the flat is half way up, it reveals Dave on his knees with a tool box, fiddling with something. His trousers have slipped down to reveal the crack in his bottom. Horrified to discover that he is in full view of the audience, he tries to sneak off stage

(Going upstage) What are you doing, Dave?
DAVE It was a bit wonky, I had an idea how to fix it. I'll just check it. *(He indicates above to have the flat dropped)* Here, Jo...

The flat flies in smartly, obscures him from view

JO So, everything's now under control, ladies and gentlemen — Mr Beaumont... Miss Brewster, if you're ready to continue... Act One, Scene One.

The flat falls with a crash right over Jo, who is unharmed as she stands in the open doorway. Simon and Phyllida still stand well out of the way

PHYLLIDA *(shrieking)* I could have been killed!
JO *(to herself)* We couldn't get that lucky.
SIMON Could I just say ... if there's too much tension, I do tend to lose my voice.
DAVE *(still busy with his tools)* I think I can see what the problem is now.
JO Touch it and die, Dave.

Jo exits to the prompt corner

DAVE Have I done something to annoy you?
SIMON *(moving towards the prompt corner and staying there)* Jo, I don't want to be difficult, but this is a very important evening for me.

The others carry on

(Waving discreetly to someone in the stalls; mouthing) Sorry!
PHYLLIDA *(slightly louder, moving downstage to ensure attention)* I could have been killed you know.

Jo enters with a pencil

JO Dave, get a chair for Miss Brewster.

Dave exits L

(Playing nervously with the pencil; to the audience) I'm so sorry we've had another slight hold up, but I'm confident...(she snaps the pencil in half)...that our celebrated cast of fine Shakespearean performers, are now ready to...

Dave walks behind her with a chair

DAVE They're not coming.

JO What?
DAVE I've been trying to tell you — they're not here.
JO How many of them are not here?
DAVE Apart from Phyllida and Simon?

Jo nods

  All of them.
JO Where are they?
DAVE In *The Dog and Trumpet. (Or local reference)*
JO How long have they been there?
DAVE Since yesterday.
JO Let me get this straight. Sixteen members of our cast are in the pub?
DAVE Fifteen actually. Old Mr Mackenzie — you know, Mustardseed — he's here, but he passed out in his dressing-room.
JO *(swinging the chair around towards Phyllida)* Miss Brewster!
PHYLLIDA *(with less confidence; sinking into her chair)* I could have been killed you know.
JO You've been telling the cast how to act again, haven't you?
PHYLLIDA One or two tiny...
SIMON ...hours...
PHYLLIDA ... pointers.
JO *(under Simon and Phyllida's dialogue)* Dave, go and get Mr Barker.
DAVE Who?
JO The Front of House Manager.
DAVE Where from?
JO The Front of House, you fool.

Dave jumps down off the stage

  No, Dave ... Dave ... Dave — the other side.
DAVE Sorry.

Instead of going round, Dave goes through the audience to the other side of the house and exits

JO *(to the audience)* I'm terribly sorry.
SIMON *(sweetly, moving towards Phyllida)* Not that I blame you. You of all people know there is always room for improvement.

PHYLLIDA I was merely thinking of the production and trying to make some simple improvements. *(She begins to collapse in tears)*

JO Off, please Simon. Get her off.

PHYLLIDA As usual, I see I have been completely misunderstood. Everyone's been beastly.

Simon moves to her side

JO *(to the audience)* I'm terrible sorry. Obviously we won't be able to continue this evening. *(To Simon)* Off, please.

PHYLLIDA *(to Simon)* This has never happened to me before.

JO *(to the audience)* This has never actually happened to me before.

SIMON Big breaths.

Simon leads Phyllida R

PHYLLIDA I could have been killed you know.

SIMON I've got some Rescue Remedy in my bag. *(He reaches into the wings for a bag from which he produces a variety of medicaments and a towel to drape around his neck)*

JO Strictly speaking, I think it's called a "technical... er...indisposition of the entire company". But it's not a problem — you will be getting your money back. I think the trick here, is to hold your ticket stubs up in the air... *(holding her arms up in the air)*... and then from the various exits in the building...*(demonstrating with arm movements, like an air stewardess)*... they will be gathered up and then you will get all your money back.

Felix enters from the back of the stalls, arguing with Dave

Ooh, Mr Barker — I'd like a word with you, please.

Felix climbs on the stage wearing a full dinner suit with a garish bow tie and matching cummerbund. A portable phone sticks out of one jacket pocket and a copy of the "Racing Post" sticks out of the other. He holds an open packet of crisps. He is followed by Dave, who stands and waits in case anybody needs him

FELIX What the hell is going on?

JO This is Mr Felix Barker, ladies and gentlemen. He's the Front of House Manager and he will be giving you all your money back. *(She starts a round of applause)*

Felix turns and registers the audience

FELIX *(shoving the crisps into his pocket)* Just a second, folks. *(He puts his hand up to protect his eyes)* Do we need all these lights? *(To the audience)* Two seconds... Jo, Jo, come here.

JO *(to the audience, walking across to Felix)* All your money back. Every penny.

FELIX *(grabbing Jo)* Money back? Have you lost your mind?

JO No. I've lost my cast.

Felix indicates R, *where Simon and Phyllida are busy in the wings with the rescue remedy*

FELIX And Phyllida and Simon, what are they — chopped liver?

JO Close. Actors. Two of them. That's "T" "W" "O", Felix. Two. That's two here, and sixteen in the snug of *The Dog and Trumpet*. *(Or local reference)*

DAVE Mr Mackenzie's in his dressing-room, but I can't get him to come round.

FELIX
              (together) Thank you, Dave.
JO

DAVE Apparently his last words were "I'm ready to go on — what's the play?".

JO Thanks, Dave. So, two actors to play eighteen parts. You sort it out.

Jo exits to the prompt corner

FELIX *(moving to prompt corner)* You're the Stage Manager, you ought to be able to do something. What is it we always say in the theatre?

Jo pops out

JO Where's my money?

Jo exits

FELIX No! The show must go on! *(He moves R)* Miss Brewster, I appeal to you.

PHYLLIDA *(sitting on her chair)* Not even on a dark night.

FELIX Mr Beaumont...!

SIMON Well, I would never knowingly let my public down.

FELIX *(grabbing Simon round the neck, dragging him L)* Good, good. Now we're cooking. *(Still holding Simon, he turns to the prompt corner)* Jo — who are the understudies?

Jo enters

JO *(consulting her prompt copy)* Well ... er, there's me. And then there's, er... me. I guess it's me mostly.

FELIX *(dropping Simon)* That's it?

JO This isn't the RSC you know. It's subsidized rep. *(Or local reference)* For two hundred pounds a week I stage manage, I understudy all the parts and I'm available in case Juliet Stevenson falls sick in *Death and the Maiden. (Or local reference)*

Jo exits to the prompt corner

PHYLLIDA I refuse to share the stage with an untrained midget.

Felix and Simon sense trouble

Jo enters slowly

JO *(smiling, advancing on Phyllida)* Oh fussy, are we, now? This from a woman who played a corpse in *Casualty.*

Phyllida leaps up and towers over Jo, who stands her ground

Dave appears in the upper portal

DAVE *(declaiming as Ophelia)*
    "Then up he rose, and donn'd his clothes,
      And dupp'd the chamber door;
    Let in the maid, that out a maid
      Never departed more." *(A small bow)*

FELIX Fabulous, Dave! *(He moves upstage to Dave)* You could use Dave.

DAVE *(jumping down to the stage)* I've been studying backstage.

SIMON *(clapping slowly, moving R)* Bravo! A magnificent performance.

Jo sits on the step. Felix stands beside her and, unheard by the audience, badgers her to continue with the play

Phyllida and I will do the Dream, while Dave weaves in and out pretending to be Hamlet's girlfriend.

DAVE *(over enthusiastic)* I can do the Dream. It's my favourite. I know it backwards.

PHYLLIDA That's pretty much how the rest of the cast knew it.

JO *(looking at Phyllida furiously, getting up and moving to Dave)* All right ... all right. Dave — you'll do.

DAVE What really? Can I really? You're not just kidding?

JO You're in, Dave.

Dave moves to stand between Simon and Phyllida, squeezing them enthusiastically round the shoulders. Phyllida is appalled

FELIX *(moving to exit through the house)* You're practically there. Simon, Phyllida, Dave, Jo...

JO And you.

FELIX *(stopping in his tracks)* Oh no...

JO Oh yes. If you think this is such a good idea, you take a part — or two. *(She moves to the prompt corner)*

FELIX *(following Jo)* I couldn't possibly — I've never appeared on a stage before...

JO *(turning on Felix)* And I suppose Dave's Laurence Olivier.

Jo exits

DAVE *(sitting on Phyllida's chair)* Well — given time.

PHYLLIDA This is absurd.

FELIX I am strictly administration.

Jo enters with the prompt book and walks to R

Felix follows her

DAVE But Miss Brewster, we wouldn't be doing this if you hadn't upset the rest of the cast and made them walk out.

JO Dave comes to us straight from the diplomatic corps. Stand by stage right, please.

Jo exits R

FELIX And I'm shy.
PHYLLIDA I have never been so insulted.

Jo enters

JO *(crossing to the prompt corner)* You want to get out more.

Jo exits

SIMON Phyllida — maybe it's up to us, the real professionals, to rally the amateur troops.

Jo enters with a script and stands C

FELIX *(moving to Jo)* When I said "the show must go on", it was not my intention to put it there personally.
DAVE Shall I collect the ticket stubs so you can give them their money back, Mr Barker?
FELIX *(eyeing the audience for a long moment)* Shit...! Where do I get my costume?
JO So, let's see — five of us to play eighteen parts. Piece of cake ... *(she sits)* ... just need to find another thirteen people.
DAVE There's always Alex, backstage.
JO Oh no, he's been ... *(she mimes smoking a joint)* ... he's gone ... *(she mimes "out of it")*
SIMON *(moving to Jo)* Some of us will have to double up.
FELIX Not me. Just a small part.
JO *(looking at Felix's crotch)* So I've heard. Two seconds, ladies and gentlemen. Cast — prompt corner, now!

Jo gets up and exits to the prompt corner, followed by Simon

FELIX *(dialling on his portable phone)* Yeah... hallo, Clive? Did you get it? Good. That's ten to one on Cissy Fairfax.

Felix exits

DAVE *(picking up Phyllida's chair)* Come on, Miss Brewster, it's going to be fun.

Dave exits

Phyllida starts to follow and then realizing she is alone on stage, turns to the audience

PHYLLIDA My dear friends, thank you for your patience in what are clearly trying times. I feel moved to speak to you at this emotional impasse, for you... we... are about to embark on a great theatrical experience and — thank you but no, I am not just referring to my own performance. For though your collective eye will naturally wish to feast upon the shining light that is my talent, I beg your indulgence of my fellow, would-be thespians — particularly the dwarf. Whatever adverse circumstances have created this predicament — and I feel wounded by the aspersions which have been cast upon the still waters of my good intentions — make no mistake, we shall give you a show. *(She moves to exit, UL)*

From the back of the house, the sound of solo clapping is heard as Tom Brindle comes through the audience to the stage

TOM Bullseye. Bloody brilliant. *(Clapping and calling her name like a chant)* Phyllida! Phyllida!

She pauses and turns

Phyllie, it's me. *(He moves down the aisle towards her)* I bet you're surprised to see me.
PHYLLIDA Tom! What are you doing here?
TOM *(leaping on stage)* Don't be cross.
PHYLLIDA I am not "cross".

Jo enters UL, *with a pile of scripts, followed by Simon*

TOM *(putting his arms around Phyllida)* Phyllie! We're meant for each other. You can't deny it.

JO Great, you found someone else.

Dave and Felix enter partly dressed in costume for Act I, Scene 1

TOM Hi! Tom Brindle — Deputy Head, PE — St Joe's for Girls. I'm her other half.

PHYLLIDA He was.

TOM Yeah, well... I expect Phyllie's mentioned me.

JO Do you know this play? *(She shows Tom a script)*

PHYLLIDA He's only a ...

TOM Natch.

PHYLLIDA You do?

TOM Sure. All those hours in bed going over your lines — remember you said I'd make a great Bottom 'cos I'm hung like a don——

PHYLLIDA — he'll be fine.

JO Right, listen up, everyone. *(She opens the script and looks at her watch)* Oh God, look at the time. Right, let's just worry about the first scene first. Phyllida, over here ... turn round ... *(She measures herself against Phyllida)* Oh yes, you are taller — you be Helena and I'll take Hermia. Simon ...

SIMON ... the Duke, of course — but I could play anything. *(To Tom)* Do you know, in a recent TIE production I played every part of the body and——

JO *(indicating Dave and Tom)* You two boys, Demetrius and Lysander — doesn't matter which.

DAVE Bottom! Please let me play Bottom.

JO We'll worry about the other parts later.

FELIX *(moving to exit)* I'm out of here.

JO And you, Felix — Egeus ... *(She throws him a script)*

FELIX *(catching the script)* Who?

JO Let's get on with this if we're going to do it, but I want to make it quite clear from the beginning that whatever's happened, this is still a professional show and therefore under no circumstances am I doing any snogging.

Tom goes to lead Phyllida off, but she shakes him away and strides to the wings. He follows

Simon starts to exit, then pauses to listen

FELIX I'm shaking. The lines are a complete blur.
JO *(indicating the audience)* It's not too late to give them their money
back.
FELIX Suddenly everything is crystal clear.

Jo and Dave move to raise the fallen flat back into position

SIMON *(taking Felix off)* Centre yourself. Reach down for that inner
calm. Big breaths.

They exit together L, *Felix trying to get rid of Simon*

Dave heads off stage and returns R *to do a blast with the smoke machine*

JO *(to the audience)* I am so sorry. *(Loudly)* Tabs in. Music. Act one,
scene one. God help us.

JO TO HERMIA; DAVE TO PHILOSTRATE; FELIX TO EGEUS;
TOM TO DEMETRIUS

Scene 2

The tabs come in and music starts again. As the Curtain *rises, Mendelssohn's "Dream" music is heard and smoke drifts across the stage*

*As before, a small band of Fairies dance up through the audience and on
to the stage. The dance is not as successful as the first time and a couple
of the Fairies fight*

Unaware of the audience, Tom enters UL, *climbs up the steps wearing his
underpants and trying to get into his costume. At the top, he realizes that
he is in full view and swiftly exits* UR

In the distance a clock strikes. The Fairies disappear and a flat showing the Duke's palace flies in as Theseus (Simon) and Hippolyta (Phyllida) enter as before. The flat comes to rest with a large crash, making Phyllida and Simon jump

THESEUS (SIMON)
> *Now*, fair Hippolyta, our nuptial hour
> Draws on apace.
> Four happy days bring in another moon ——
HIPPOLYTA (PHYLLIDA) *(interrupting)*
> Four days will quickly steep themselves in night;
> Four nights will quickly dream away the time ——
THESEUS (SIMON)*(interrupting)*
> Go, Philostrate ...

Pause, nothing happens. Simon looks panic stricken to prompt corner. Voices come from DR

DAVE *(off)* Who's Philostrate?
JO *(off)* You'll have to do it.
DAVE *(off)* I can't — I'm Lysander. I can't do both.
JO *(off)* He doesn't speak.

> *Dave is pushed on,* DL, *wearing a false beard and carrying a small Union Jack. He stands for a moment facing Simon, then turns uncertainly*

DAVE Philostrate. *(To the audience, lifting up the beard)* Not really, it's me, Dave. *(He waves the Union Jack)*

Simon takes a deep breath. Phyllida imperceptibly shakes her head

THESEUS (SIMON)
> Go, Philostrate,
> Stir up the Athenian youth to merriments.
DAVE *(at a loss)* Righto.

Dave waves the flag, then notices Simon discreetly indicating that he should move L,*which he does awkwardly, waving his flag as he goes*

SIMON Why, here comes Hermia, Demetrius *and Lysander.* That's you, Dave.

Dave panics and exits L

DAVE TO LYSANDER

Hermia (Jo), Demetrius (Tom), and Egeus (Felix) enter R. *Felix and Jo are carrying scripts, Jo is wearing a diaphanous gown which she finds a bit embarrassing*

Phyllida goes to take up her posing position in the open portal

THESEUS (SIMON)
    Good Egeus. What's the news with thee?
FELIX *(scanning the script)* Damned if I know.

Jo points out the right place

EGEUS (FELIX)
    Full of vexation ——
SIMON Speak up.
FELIX Is it too quiet?
SIMON *I* can't hear you.
EGEUS (FELIX)
    Full of vexation come I, with complaint
    Against my child, my daughter Hermia.
    Stand forth, Demetrius!

Tom smiles winningly at the audience

        Pause. My noble Lord,
    This man hath my consent to marry her.
    Stand forth, Lysander!

Lysander (Dave) rushes on with his script

    And, my gracious Duke,
    This hath bewitched the bosom of my child.
    She will not consent to marry with Demetrius,
    I beg the ancient privilege of Athens two hundred:

JO That's the line number, we don't read that bit.
EGEUS (FELIX)
    I beg the ancient privilege of Athens
    As she is mine, I may dispose of her
    Which shall be either to this gentleman or to her death.
FELIX I'm out of here. *(He goes to exit* R*)*

Theseus speaks, Jo pulls Felix back on stage

THESEUS (SIMON)
    What say you, Hermia? Be advised, fair maid:
    To you your father should be as a god;
    Demetrius is a worthy gentleman.
HERMIA (JO)
    (reading) So is Lysander. *(She kneels)*
    But I beseech your grace that I may know
    The worst that may befall me in this case
    If I refuse to wed Demetrius.
THESEUS (SIMON)
    Either to die the death, or to abjure
    For ever the society of men.
    Take time to pause, and by the next new moon
    The sealing day betwixt my love and me
    Upon that day either prepare to die
    For disobedience to your father's will,
    Or else to wed Demetrius, as he would,
    Or on Diana's altar to protest
    For aye austerity and single life.
DEMETRIUS (TOM) *(gearing up for his big moment)*
    Relent, sweet Hermia; and, Lysander, yield
    Thy crazed title to my certain right.

Thrilled that he has remembered his lines, Tom looks to the audience for
approval — he does athletic knee bends. Dave moves L *to speak to him,*
notices the knee bends and copies uncertainly

LYSANDER (DAVE)
    You have her father's love, Demetrius —
    Let me have Hermia's. Do you marry *him*.
TOM What?

Egeus (Felix) moves to speak to Lysander. Dave encourages him to join in the knee bends

EGEUS (FELIX)
  Scornful Lysander.

Felix scurries back to his original position. Tom and Dave stop the knee bends

DAVE No. Come back.

Dave follows Felix and stands in front of him, delivering his lines with his back to the audience. As he speaks, Jo and Simon subtly try and get him to turn around

LYSANDER (DAVE) *(reading in what he thinks is a Shakespearean rhythm)*
  I am, my Lord, as well derived as he,
  As well possessed. My love is more than his,
  My fortunes every way as fairly ranked —
  If not with vantage — as Demetrius'.
  And — which is more than all these boasts can be —
  I am beloved of beauteous Hermia. *(He finally turns)*
  Demetrius made love to Helena,
  And won her soul.
THESEUS (SIMON)
  Demetrius, come; And come, Egeus.

Phyllida storms off UL. *Tom exits* DL

  You shall go with me.
  I have some private schooling for you both.

Felix exits L

Theseus turns to Hermia (Jo), who is paying no attention as she has realized the hot lights are making her sweat. She indicates this to Dave

        For you, fair Hermia, look you arm yourself
    To fit your fancies to your father's will;
    Come, my Hippolyta.

The portal shuts. Simon realizes she has gone

> What cheer, my love?
> Demetrius and Egeus...

FELIX *(off)* What?

Felix and Tom rush back on

THESEUS (SIMON)
> *(pushing them off stage)* ... I must confer with you
> Of something nearly that concerns yourselves.

FELIX On, off, on, off — make up your mind, you little twerp.

They exit

SIMON TO QUINCE; PHYLLIDA TO HELENA; FELIX TO SNUG

DAVE Shall we carry on? You look lovely.

LYSANDER (DAVE)
> How now, my love?...

JO Not yet, I have to cry first.

She has a go at crying, then beckons to Dave who kneels next to her

LYSANDER (DAVE)
> How now, my love? Why is your cheek so pale?
> How chance the roses there do fade so fast?

Hermia (Jo) gets up awkwardly, followed by Dave

HERMIA (JO)
> Belike for want of rain, which I could well
> Beteem them from the tempest of my eyes.

She turns to face Dave, but his script blocks her view as he holds it right in front of her face

LYSANDER (DAVE)
> Hear me, Hermia:
> I have a widow aunt...

JO I can't see you.
DAVE Sorry.
LYSANDER (DAVE)
    From Athens is her house remote seven leagues;
    There, gentle Hermia, may I marry thee;
    And to that place the sharp Athenian law
    Cannot pursue us.
    If thou lovest me, then
    Steal forth thy father's house tomorrow night,
    And in the wood, a league without the town —
    There will I stay for thee.
HERMIA (JO)
    Tomorrow truly will I meet with thee.
LYSANDER (DAVE)
    Keep promise, love. *(He moves to kiss her)*

Jo is appalled. Phyllida clears her throat loudly, off stage

    Look — here comes Helena.

Helena (Phyllida) enters L *with a script*

HERMIA (JO)
    God speed, fair Helena! *(Confidently)* Whither away.
    (She wonders whether what she's just said was really written as an
    insult. She moves to sit with Helena on the step C)

Phyllida has decided to play Helena with a girlie lisp

HELENA (PHYLLIDA) *(half-referring to the script)*
    Call you me fair? That "fair" again unsay.
    Demetrius loves your fair. O happy fair!
    Your eyes are lodestars ...

Jo mouths "lodestars" to Dave, mimicking Phyllida's delivery

                         ... and your tongue's sweet air
    More tunable than lark to shepherd's ear
    When wheat is green ...

Jo mouths to Dave again

                       ... when hawthorn buds appear
    Sickness is catching.

Jo keels over with silent laughter

    O, were favour so,
    Yours would I catch, fair Hermia, ere I go.
    My ear should catch your voice, my eye your eye,
    My tongue should catch your tongue's sweet melody.
    O teach me how you look, and with what art
    You sway the motion of Demetrius' heart.
JO *(sitting up)* I don't know where to begin really.
HERMIA (JO) *(mimicking Phyllida's voice)*
    I frown upon him, yet he loves me still.
    The more I hate, the more he follows me.
HELENA (PHYLLIDA) *(furious, reverting to her own voice)*
    The more I love, the more he hateth me.
HERMIA (JO)
    His folly, Helena, is no fault of mine.
HELENA (PHYLLIDA)
    None but your beauty. Would that fault were mine!
PHYLLIDA I'm sorry, these lines are making me unwell. *(She stands and moves to the prompt corner)*

    Tom appears

Have you seen these two? It's like working with the Krankies!

    Tom calms her, then exits

TOM TO FLUTE

HERMIA (JO) *(normally; dragging Phyllida back to* c, *but Phyllida continues to look to the prompt corner)*
    Take comfort. Demetrius no more shall see my face.
    Lysander and myself will fly this place.
LYSANDER (DAVE)
    Helen...

(No response, so he hits Phyllida on the head with his script to get her attention)
>... to you our minds we will unfold.
>Tomorrow night, through Athens gates have we devised to steal.

HERMIA (JO)
>And in the wood, Lysander and myself shall meet
>And thence from Athens turn away our eyes
>To seek new friends and stranger companies.
>Farewell, sweet playfellow. *(Hugging the furious Phyllida)*
>Pray thou for us;
>And good luck grant thee thy Demetrius.
>Keep word, Lysander. We must starve our sight
>From lover's food till morrow deep midnight.

LYSANDER (DAVE)
>I will, my Hermia.

He moves to kiss Jo, but she stops him

JO I told you — no snogging.

She exits L

JO TO SNOUT

LYSANDER (DAVE)
>Helena, adieu!
>*(As if he has a whole speech to deliver)*
>As you on him, Demetrius dote on you...
>*(He checks his script and realizes he has finished)*

DAVE I've finished!

PHYLLIDA Get off.

DAVE *(rushing off* R*)* I've done that first bit.

Dave exits

DAVE TO BOTTOM

HELENA (PHYLLIDA) *(moving down* C, *closing her script)*
>Ere Demetrius looked on Hermia's eyne

He hailed down oaths that he was only mine,
And when this hail some heat from Hermia felt,
So he dissolved, and showers of oaths did melt.
I will go tell him of fair Hermia's flight.
Then to the wood will he tomorrow night
Pursue her; and for this intelligence
If I have thanks it is a dear expense.

Phyllida exits L, bumping into Jo who wears her cans and carries the prompt script and revolve control box

PHYLLIDA TO STARVELING

Scene 3

NB. For this scene, Felix continues to read from the script, Jo uses her prompt copy, everyone else is off the book

JO Stand by in the flies for flying cue two, LX cues eight and follow ons, stand by on the revolve. Go! Brilliant.

Jo exits

The revolve turns and the palace flat flies out. Flute the Bellows Mender (Tom) sits on the top step, eating a McDonald's. Quince the Carpenter (Simon), holding a scroll of the Pyramus and Thisbe play, stands in front of him explaining the next scene. Snug the Joiner (Felix) sits on a lower step trying to learn his part

Bottom (Dave) enters R, pulling an old-fashioned props basket on wheels with "HISP" on the side. He steps on to the revolve as it starts to move and keeps walking, getting nowhere. He keeps trying to signal to Jo to stop the revolve. It eventually stops abruptly, having gone too far round one way, and turns back again with Dave desperately trying to stop it

SIMON So is that clear?
TOM What other play?
QUINCE (SIMON)
       Is all our company here?

JO *(off)* PHYLLIDA!

Jo enters as Snout, still carrying her prompt copy, with her cans round her neck, mouths "sorry" to Simon and sits on the steps, R, as Tom speaks

TOM Mac Attack. Anybody hungry?

Tom eats the burger as Dave fiddles with the props

FELIX What?
SIMON Amateurs!
QUINCE (SIMON) *(yokel accent)* Here is the scroll of every man's name which is thought fit through all Athens to play in our interlude before the Duke and the Duchess on his wedding day at night. Our play is *The Most Lamentable Comedy and Most Cruel Death of Pyramus and Thisbe.*
TOM Time out. Sorry, are we doing a different play now?
SIMON There's a play at the end of this play. We play the actors in the play who entertain the lords and ladies who watch the play.
TOM Tricky this acting lark.

Starveling (Phyllida) enters, L

QUINCE (SIMON)
        You, Nick Bottom...

Dave looks up from the props basket, he wears a Groucho Marx moustache made from gaffa tape

SIMON Dave, what is that?
DAVE What's what? What? *(Looking around for disaster)*
SIMON That ... that strip of sticky back plastic which you are sporting on your top lip.
DAVE *(confidently)* Oh no, that's character acting. Building a character. This scene, you see — completely different character. Older man. Facial hair. I've got no make-up. That's natural.

Simon looks at him long and hard, then rips the tape from Dave's top lip. Everyone reacts

QUINCE (SIMON)
    You, Nick Bottom, are set down for Pyramus.
BOTTOM (DAVE) *(fake Welsh accent)*
    What is Pyramus? — a lover or a tyrant?
SIMON Stop. The lip was bad enough. What is that noise that's coming
    out from underneath it?
DAVE I thought I'd do a West Country accent for this part.
SIMON You sounded Lithuanian.
TOM I thought it was very good. Better than the one I was going to do.

All agree

QUINCE (SIMON) *(sighing, continuing)*
    Pyramus is a lover that kills himself.
ALL Ooooh!
BOTTOM (DAVE) *(fake Geordie accent)*
    That will ask some tears in the true performing of it. If I do it, let the
    audience look to their eyes! I will move storms.
QUINCE (SIMON)
    Francis Flute, the bellows-mender?
FLUTE (TOM) *(with terrible West Country accent)*
    Here, Peter Quince.
QUINCE (SIMON)
    You must take Thisbe on you.
FLUTE (TOM)
    What be Thisbe? — a wandering knight?
    (He looks around for approval for the accent)
QUINCE (SIMON)
    It is the lady that Pyramus must love.
FLUTE (TOM)
    Nay faith, let not me play a woman.
TOM I'm not wearing a frock — I've got my reputation to think of.
PHYLLIDA That shouldn't take long.
BOTTOM (DAVE) *(beginning to get the hang of the West Country
    accent)*
    Let me play Thisbe too. I'll speak in a monstrous little voice. "Ah
    Pyramus, my lover dear; thy Thisbe dear and lady dear".
QUINCE (SIMON) *(cross)*
    No, no; you must play Pyramus; and Flute, you Thisbe. Robin
    Starveling, the tailor?

STARVELING (PHYLLIDA) *(uninterested)*
   Here, Peter Quince.

Quince (Simon) hands her the scroll. She holds her outfit away from her body

PHYLLIDA I swear something's died in this costume.
QUINCE (SIMON)
   Tom Snout, the tinker?
SNOUT (JO) *(reading from the prompt copy, West Country accent)*
   'Ere Peter Quince. Ooh aargh, ooh aargh, ooh aargh.
DAVE What's that?
JO That's West Country, if you do that — "ooh aargh".
QUINCE (SIMON)
   Snug, the Joiner, you the lion's part;
SNUG (FELIX) *(reading, in a weird accent)*
   Have you the lion's part written? Pray you, if it be, give it me; for
   I am slow of study.
QUINCE (SIMON)
   It's nothing but roaring.
ALL Roar!
BOTTOM (DAVE)
   Let me play the lion too. I will roar that I will make the Duke say
   "let him roar again; let him roar again".
QUINCE (SIMON)
   You can play no part but Pyramus. Here are your parts...
   I desire you to con them by tomorrow night...
SNOUT (JO) As soon as that.
QUINCE (SIMON)
                 ... and meet me in the palace wood ...
FLUTE (TOM) Oh, I know— the wood by the palace.
QUINCE (SIMON)
   ... a mile without the town ...
SNOUT (JO) Better take our bicycles, then. *(Closing the lid of the props
   basket, she moves to take it off R)*
QUINCE (SIMON) *(exasperated)*
   There will we rehearse.
FELIX Jo, we need to talk. I probably should have told you before,
   but ——
JO Later, Felix. I'm a bit busy.

Jo exits. Dave exits L *to do the scene change*

TOM *(throwing his burger wrapper at Simon's head)* Don't worry, mate. Keep it up! We're on a winning team.

Tom exits L, *leering at Phyllida*

Phyllida crosses to R

SIMON *(exhausted)* Phyllida, how could you ever have gone with a man like that — he's an animal.
PHYLLIDA Exactly, darling ... *(she indicates the size of Tom's private parts by holding up either end of the rolled up scroll)* ... like a stallion on a stud farm.

Phyllida exits R

SIMON *(to the audience)* Enough said.

Simon exits L

FELIX TO OBERON; PHYLLIDA TO TITANIA; TOM TO PEASE-BLOSSOM; SIMON TO MUSTARDSEED

Mendelssohn music as Dave and Jo do the scene change, then exit

DAVE TO LYSANDER; JO TO PUCK WITH HARNESS

SCENE 4

NB. The flying scenes work best if it appears that Dave is controlling it all with his looped fly rope

Smoke. Forest transformation. Music. Four Fairies dance on, circle the stage and as they come back towards the audience, Simon (from L*) and Tom (from* R*) join them dressed as Peaseblossom and Mustardseed, complete with tights and tutus. As they dance, Simon surreptitiously checks on Tom's physical endowments and is shocked to discover that Phyllida has not exaggerated. Tom is very athletic and does the high jumps* *with ease. At the end of the dance, everyone exits*

Peaseblossom (Tom) and Mustardseed (Simon) enter R, *awkwardly
carrying Titania (Phyllida) who wears a long, flowing fairy wig. They
position her on the banks. The Changeling Boy follows them on and sits
with Titania. Simon and Tom crouch behind them in attendance. Oberon
(Felix) enters* L, *briefly studies his script, then tosses it into the wings*

OBERON (FELIX)
   Ill met by moonlight, proud Titania!
TITANIA (PHYLLIDA)
   What, jealous Oberon? Fairies, skip hence.

   Tom and Simon exit R, *but peep round a column*

   I have forsworn his bed and company.
OBERON (FELIX)
   Tarry, rash *(pronounced like Chinese food)* won-ton!
JO *(off, correct pronunciation)* Wanton!
OBERON (FELIX)
   Wanton. Am not I thy lord?
   Why should Titania cross her Oberon?
   I do but beg a little changeling boy
   To be my henchman.
   (He tries to be elegant as he sits, but fails)
TITANIA (PHYLLIDA)
   Set your heart at rest.
   The fairy land buys not the child of me.
   His mother was a votaress of my order,
   But she, being mortal, of that boy did die,
   And for her sake do I rear up her boy;
   And for her sake I will not part with him.
OBERON (FELIX) *(toying with her wig)*
   How long within this wood intend you to stay?
TITANIA (PHYLLIDA)
   Perchance till after Theseus' wedding day.
   If you will patiently dance in our round

Felix realizes part of Titania's wig is caught round his finger

And see our moonlight revels, go with us.
If not, shun me, and I will spare your haunts.
OBERON (FELIX)
Give me that boy and I will go with thee.
(He gestures with his hand and the wig flies off. He is mortified)
TITANIA (PHYLLIDA)
Not for thy fairy kingdom! Fairies!

Peaseblossom (Tom) and Mustardseed (Simon) come forward to carry Titania away . The Changeling Boy follows

Away! We shall chide downright if I longer stay.
FELIX Miss Brewster, I'm so sorry.
PHYLLIDA Give me back my wig.

Phyllida grabs it from him as the Fairies carry her off inelegantly, Tom facing her and holding her legs either side of him

Tom! No, Tom, stop that.

Titania exits with her train

TOM TO DEMETRIUS; PHYLLIDA TO HELENA; SIMON TO QUINCE

OBERON (FELIX) *(standing up)*
Well, go thy way.
Thou shalt not from this grove
Till I torment thee for this injury.
(Looking R) My gentle Puck, come hither.

Dave enters L, walking backwards looking up to the flies, holding a thick fly rope

DAVE Two ticks! Two ticks! It'll be worth the wait. I've rigged it all up...
JO *(off)* Dave? Dave — I don't feel well. I've changed my mind. I want to come DO...WN....

As she speaks, Dave pulls the rope and Puck (Jo) flies in L *to* R *somersaulting, coming to rest upside down by Oberon's head. She no longer wears her glasses*

DAVE Brilliant! Here, have this.

He thrusts a paper bag into her hand as she turns up the right way. Jo is sick into the bag and hands it to Felix

   Don't worry, you're in safe hands. I'm in charge.

Dave stands R, *vigilant with his flying rope. Felix hands Dave the sick bag. Dave throws it into the wings*

FELIX (*sarcastic*) When you're ready, Jo. Only I have got to be
   somewhere at half-eight.

Jo waves him on

OBERON (FELIX)
      Puck...
PUCK (JO) (*groaning*) Yeah?
OBERON (FELIX)
      ...thou rememberest
      Since once I sat upon a promontory
      And heard a mermaid on a dolphin's back
      Uttering such dulcet and harmonious breath
      That the rude sea grew civil at her song,
      And certain stars shot madly from their spheres
      To hear the sea maid's music?
JO No. I don't remember that at all.

Felix grabs her towards him by the front of her costume, so her legs flip up

FELIX Play the game.
OBERON (FELIX)
      That very time I saw
      Flying between the cold moon and the earth
      Cupid all armed. A certain aim he took

At a fair vestal throned by the west,
And loosed his loveshaft smartly from his bow.

With the last line, he makes a big gesture with his left arm, which sends Jo flying off left into the flies, and causes Dave to be hauled straight up on his rope, balancing precariously with one foot in a toe loop

Jo exits

FELIX *(looking* L*)* Can't she go any lower? I'm getting a terrible crick in my neck.

As he speaks, Felix turns, sees Dave and goes to pull him down

As Dave comes down, Jo flies in low over the stage and knocks Felix over

Jo puts her hand out to help Felix up. As he grabs it, she flips over. He stands up, puts her back in the right position and they both pose with her on his left shoulder, as if nothing has happened

OBERON (FELIX)
It fell upon a little western flower,
Before, milk white; now purple with love's wound;
And maidens call it "love in idleness".
Fetch me that flower — the herb I showed thee once.
The juice of it on sleeping eyelids laid
Will make or man or woman madly dote
Upon the next live creature that it sees.
Fetch me this herb and be thou here again
Ere the leviathan can swim a league.
PUCK (JO)
I'll put a girdle round about the earth
In forty minutes!
JO Slowly, Dave!

Dave pulls on the rope

Dave...*(She starts to judder* L*)* You can go a bit faster than that — I told the man forty minutes, you don't want to make it an hour and a half.

Dave pulls the rope the other way and Jo moves R, *very fast, flying off into the wings and taking Dave with her*

OBERON (FELIX)
    Having once this juice
    I'll watch Titania when she is asleep,
    And drop the liquor of it in her eyes.
    The next thing then she, waking, looks upon —
    She shall pursue it with the soul of love.
    And ere I take this charm from off her sight —
    I'll make her render up her page to me.
DEMETRIUS (TOM) *(off)*
    I love thee not, therefore pursue me not.
OBERON (FELIX)
    But who comes here? *(Confidently)* I am invisible ...

Felix turns to go, then turns back to the audience in disgust if they haven't believed him

FELIX Use your imaginations.
OBERON (FELIX)
    ... And I will overhear their conference. *(He moves upstage)*

Demetrius (Tom) enters R *and hides* L *until Helena (Phyllida) crosses without noticing him, and exits* L.*Oberon disappears and Tom wonders at the magic of the forest*

NB. For the original production, the actor wore a cloak with a pair of false shoulders. He turned his back on the audience and attached the shoulders to a mechanism hidden in the set. This allowed Oberon to disappear through a lycra panel with a split in it, while his cloak remained apparently standing, masking his exit. Once the actor had successfully left the stage, the mechanism was withdrawn and the cloak fell to the floor

Phyllida enters

TOM *(sitting on the bank)* Phyllida, I don't know if I can do this bit.
PHYLLIDA What is the problem?
TOM I don't want to say nasty things to you.
PHYLLIDA Cut the sentimentality, Tom. You pushed your way in here,

now deal with the consequences. And remember this— when I deliver
my lines, I am only acting.

TOM But Phyllida ... I love you!

PHYLLIDA Speak.

DEMETRIUS (TOM)

> Where is Lysander, and fair Hermia?
>
> Thou toldest me they were stolen unto this wood.
>
> Get thee gone, and follow me no more.

HELENA (PHYLLIDA) *(pushing Demetrius on to his back)*

> You draw me, you hard-hearted adamant!

DEMETRIUS (TOM) *(pushing Helena on to her back and kneeling astride her)*

> Do I entice you? Do I speak you fair?
>
> Or rather do I not in plainest truth
>
> Tell you I do not nor I cannot love you?

HELENA (PHYLLIDA)

> And even for that do I love you the more.

Demetrius stands and Helena grabs his leg

> I am your spaniel; and, Demetrius,
>
> The more you beat me I will fawn on you.
>
> Use me but as your spaniel: spurn me, strike me,
>
> Neglect me, lose me; only give me leave,
>
> Unworthy as I am, to follow you.

DEMETRIUS (TOM) *(freeing himself, running up the bank)*

> Tempt not too much the hatred of my spirit;
>
> For I am sick when I do look on thee.

HELENA (PHYLLIDA) *(following)*

> And I am sick when I look not on you.

DEMETRIUS (TOM)

> I'll run from thee and hide me in the brakes,
>
> And leave thee to the mercy of wild beasts.

HELENA (PHYLLIDA)

> The wildest hath not such a heart as you.
>
> Run when you will. The story shall be changed.

DEMETRIUS (TOM)

> Let me go;
>
> Or if thou follow me, do not believe
>
> But I shall do thee mischief in the wood.

Tom moves in close to kiss her, then throws her to the ground instead

He turns to audience with a look of triumph and exits L

HELENA (PHYLLIDA)
> I'll follow thee, and make a heaven of hell,
> To die upon the hand I love so well.

PHYLLIDA Tom?

Phyllida exits L

A stage maroon erupts R as Oberon (Felix) appears confidently L. It takes him a beat to realize the mistake, then he walks R in a temper

FELIX Dave! I said stage left.

DAVE *(off)* Sorry!

OBERON (FELIX) *(waving away the smoke and looking L)*
> Fair thee well, nymph. Ere he do leave this grove
> Thou shalt fly him, and he shall seek thy love.

Puck (Jo) enters flying with Dave behind her pulling his rope

JO Mind your head, mind your head.

She flies in low R to L with a flower. Oberon ducks as she passes over his head and catches the flat very high L

> Be right back.

Dave works the rope as she flies back down to R, coming to rest C, next to Oberon

OBERON (FELIX)
> Welcome, wanderer. Hast thou the flower there?

PUCK (JO)
> Ay, there it is. *(She hands the flower over)*

OBERON (FELIX)
> I pray thee give it me. *(He realizes he already has it)*

FELIX *(irritated)* Sit!

JO Sit, Dave.

Dave pulls the rope and with straight legs, Jo falls slowly forward instead of backwards. She looks at him, he pulls the rope the other way and she rises up again and sits down

OBERON (FELIX)
    I know a....
FELIX Dave, we're alone in the woods.
DAVE *(looking round)* Yeah, just the three of us.

Jo motions for him to exit

  It dawns on Dave what Felix meant, so he exits

OBERON (FELIX)
    I know a bank where the wild thyme blows,
    Where oxlips and the nodding violet grows,
    Quite overcanopied with luscious woodbine,
    With sweet muskroses and with eglantine.
    There sleeps Titania some time of the night,
    Lulled in these flowers with dances and delight.
    And with the juice of this I'll streak her eyes
    And make her full of hateful fantasies.

He hands Jo a flower, she gets to her feet

    Take thou some of it, and seek through this grove.

He pushes Jo upwards, she floats up gently and he stands

        A sweet Athenian lady is in love
    With a disdainful youth...

Jo comes down again, landing elegantly on Felix's outstretched hand

        ...anoint his eyes;
    But do it when the next thing he espies
    May be the lady. Thou shalt know the man
    By the Athenian garments he hath on.
    Effect it with some care, that he may prove
    More fond on her than she upon her love.
    And look thou meet me ere the first cock crow.

JO *(dropping into Felix's arms)* You're getting good at this Felix.
FELIX Thanks — only put a rocket under it, I've got an appointment.
PUCK (JO)
> Fear not, my lord; your servant shall do so.

Felix exits UL. *Dave appears* L *with aircraft batons in his hands*

DAVE You'll be all right this time — there's two of us.
JO Not Alex?
DAVE No, Tom.

Tom appears R, *holding the fly-rope*

Jo *(seeing Tom)* No, Tom doesn't know what he's doing.

Tom starts to pull the rope

> Tom, Tom — that's the wrong way.

Dave motions with his aircraft batons towards himself, but Jo flies off R
over Tom's head. He pulls the rope the other way and she appears flying
R *to* L, *knocking Dave over and grabbing the aircraft batons as she passes.
There is a terrible sound of breaking glass*

TOM How was that?
DAVE Nearly.

Jo gives a slight groan

> Give us a hand with the scene change, Tom.

JO TO HERMIA WITHOUT HARNESS

Tom and Dave do the scene change

> *Titania's double enters to take up her sleeping position*

Tom flirts with her as if it were Phyllida

> *Dave exits* L, *Tom exits* R, *leaving Titania asleep on the top step*

SCENE 5

Music

Oberon (Felix) enters UC, *holding the flower to squeeze on to Titania's eyes*

OBERON (FELIX)
>   What thou seest when thou dost wake,
>   Do it for thy true love take;
>   Love and languish for his sake.
>   Be it ounce, or cat, or bear,
>   Pard, or boar with bristled hair,
>   In thy eye that shall appear
>   When thou wakest, it is thy dear.
>   Wake when some vile thing is near!

(He squeezes the flower on Titania's eyes, there is a large squirt of water)

He exits, laughing

<u>FELIX TO SNUG</u>

Hermia (Jo) and Lysander (Dave) enter DL. *Dazed from her flying accident as Puck, Jo wears a large bandage round her head and is supported by Dave, who carries a blanket. They wander aimlessly around the stage*

JO Dave, what are we doing?
DAVE We're wandering in the wood.
LYSANDER (DAVE)
>   Fair love, you faint with wandering in the wood.

JO I think it was the blow to my head. Look ... *(She shows Dave the bump)*
DAVE Haven't you got lovely hair. *(He strokes it)*
JO Get on with it.
LYSANDER (DAVE)
>   And — to speak truth — I have forgot our way.
>   We'll rest us, Hermia...*(He lays the blanket on the ground,* L*)*

> ...if you think it good,
> And tarry for the comfort of the day.

HERMIA (JO)
> Be it so, Lysander; find you out a bed,
> For I upon this bank will rest my head.

She moves R. *Lysander (Dave) picks up the blanket and follows*

LYSANDER (DAVE)
> One turf shall serve as pillow for us both;
> One heart, one bed, two bosoms, and one truth.

He holds up the blanket to mask Jo's substitution with her double, who takes the blanket from him and pushes him away as:

> *Jo exits* R

<u>JO TO PUCK</u>

As Hermia speaks, the double wraps herself up and settles on the ground R

HERMIA (JO)
> Nay, good Lysander, for my sake, my dear,
> Lie further off yet; do not lie so near.

DAVE Can I just tuck you in?

He moves to cover Hermia and the double smacks his hand

LYSANDER (DAVE) (*moving back* L)
> Here is my bed: sleep give thee all his rest.

Ethereal music plays as they drift off to sleep, Dave taking some time to settle himself, pretending to brush his teeth and wind an imaginary alarm clock

> *Puck (Jo) enters* UC *with the flower. She comes down the bank and sits* DC

PUCK (JO)
> Through the forest have I gone,
> But Athenian found I none

On whose eyes I might approve.
This flower's force in stirring love. *(She stands)*
Night and silence.

Dave snores

Who is here?
(She moves to Lysander)
Weeds of Athens he doth wear.
This is he my master said
Despised the Athenian maid;
And here the maiden...*(moves to double)*...sleeping sound
On the dank and dirty ground.
Pretty soul...
JO *(to the audience)* Gorgeous. Personally, I think she's gorgeous.
PUCK (JO)
...she durst not lie
Near this lack-love, this kill-courtesy.
Churl, upon thy eyes I throw
All the power this charm doth owe.
(She squeezes the flower on Lysander's eyes with a great squirt of water)
When thou wakest let love forbid
Sleep his seat on thy eyelid.
So, awake when I am gone;
For I must now to Oberon.

Jo exits DL

JO TO HERMIA

Demetrius (Tom) and Helena (Phyllida) enter UR, *out of breath. Demetrius squats* C, *joined by Helena. He goes to move away, she stops him*

HELENA (PHYLLIDA)
Stay though thou kill me, sweet Demetrius!
DEMETRIUS (TOM)
I charge thee hence; and do not haunt me thus.
HELENA (PHYLLIDA)
O, wilt thou darkling leave me? Do not so!

DEMETRIUS (TOM)
>Stay, on thy peril. I alone will go.

Tom exits R

TOM TO FLUTE

HELENA (PHYLLIDA) *(collapsing to the ground)*
>O, I am out of breath in this fond chase.

Lysander moans

>But who is here? — Lysander on the ground?
>Dead or asleep? I see no blood, no wound.
>*(Kneeling next to him)*
>Lysander, if you live, good sir, awake!

LYSANDER (DAVE) *(awaking aroused)*
>And run through fire I will for thy sweet sake!
>Transparent Helena, nature shows art
>That through thy bosom ... *(He grabs her breast)*

PHYLLIDA Get off!

LYSANDER (DAVE) *(continuing to paw after her on the ground)*
>   ... makes me see thy heart.
>Where is Demetrius? O, how fit a word
>Is that vile name to perish on my sword!

HELENA (PHYLLIDA) *(trying to escape)*
>Do not say so, Lysander, say not so.
>What though he love your Hermia, lord, what though?
>Yet Hermia still loves you. Then be content.

PHYLLIDA Jo! Jo!

LYSANDER (DAVE)
>Content with Hermia? No, I do repent
>The tedious minutes I with her have spent.
>*(He holds her and turns her towards him in his arms)*
>Not Hermia but Helena I love.
>Who will not change a raven for a dove?

HELENA (PHYLLIDA) *(standing up)*
>Wherefore was I to this keen mockery born?
>When at your hands did I deserve this scorn?
>*(Pulling away from him)*

Is't not enough, is't not enough young man
That I did never — no, nor never can —
Deserve a sweet look from Demetrius' eye
But you must flout my insufficiency?

Dave does his best horny gyrations towards Phyllida

Good troth, you do me wrong — good sooth, you do —
In such disdainful manner me to woo.
But fare you well. Perforce I must confess

Dave moves in thinking he is going to get a kiss

I thought you lord of more true gentleness.

Phyllida knees him in the groin and exits L

PHYLLIDA TO STARVELING

LYSANDER (DAVE) *(almost unable to speak)*
She sees not Hermia. Hermia, sleep thou there.
And never mayst thou come Lysander near.

Dave exits L. *There is a loud shout of pain, off*

DAVE TO BOTTOM

HERMIA (JO) *(off)*
Help me, Lysander, help me!

*The double stands, holding the blanket up in front of her. As Jo speaks,
the double shakes the blanket from side to side and flaps it, to cover Jo
entering* R *and taking the blanket from her double*

HERMIA (JO)
Do thy best
To pluck this crawling serpent from my breast!
*(She shakes blanket from side to side, then drops it to reveal herself and
give a thumbs up to her double in the wings)*
Ay me, for pity! — What a dream was here!

Lysander, look how I do quake with fear!
Lysander — what removed? Lysander, lord!
Gone? No sound, no word?
No? Then I well perceive you are not nigh,
Either death or you I'll find immediately.

Jo exits R

<u>JO TO SNOUT</u>

SCENE 6

Mechanicals music

Quince (Simon) strides on DR, *without realizing that he is being followed by Flute (Tom) and Bottom (Dave)*

Simon takes a moment to adjust his costume and strike a pose as he surveys the house. He makes a tiny gesture of greeting towards the special seat in the stalls. Tom and Dave try to see who Simon is gesturing to and start waving in that direction too

DAVE *(stage whispering)* Is it your mum?
SIMON *(embarrassed)* No.
TOM Your girlfriend? She's very pretty.
SIMON It's a man, dolt.

Tom has a good look

It's Vincent Chalmers.

Tom and Dave look blank

Only Britain's foremost casting director.
DAVE *(not knowing)* Oh, him.
SIMON *(aside)* I am very hopeful... *(he smiles to the stalls)* ... that he's going to offer me a rather substantial film role. Let's get on. *(He claps his hands)*

The others enter L: Snout (Jo) with the "HISP" props basket, Starveling (Phyllida) and Snug (Felix). Everyone is now very involved in West Country yokel-acting

ALL *(except Simon and Phyllida)* Oooh aargh, ooh aargh!
QUINCE (SIMON)
> Here's a marvellous convenient place for our rehearsal.
JO It's most convenient, it's right here.

Felix takes a sword from the props basket

QUINCE (SIMON)
> This green plot shall be our stage, this hawthorn brake our tiring-house, and we will do it in action as we will do it before the Duke.
BOTTOM (DAVE)
> Peter Quince!
QUINCE (SIMON)
> What sayest thou, Bully Bottom?
BOTTOM (DAVE)
> There are things in this comedy of Pyramus and Thisbe that will never please. First, Pyramus must draw a sword to kill himself...
FELIX ...Exhibit A.
BOTTOM (DAVE)
> ...which the ladies cannot abide. How answer you that?
SNOUT (JO)
> By'r lakin, a parlous fear!
STARVELING (PHYLLIDA) *(bad accent)*
> I believe we must leave the killing out, when all is done.

All stop and stare at her

PHYLLIDA Look, you know I don't do character work.
ALL Ooh Aargh.

Jo hands Phyllida her Starveling props : a tatty stuffed dog and an old lamp

BOTTOM (DAVE)
> Not a wit.

ALL No, she's not.

DAVE No, that's my next line.

BOTTOM (DAVE)

> Not a wit. I have a device to make all well. Write me a prologue, and let the prologue seem to say we will do no harm with our swords, and that Pyramus is not killed indeed.

SNOUT (JO)

> Will not the ladies be afeard of the lion?

STARVELING (PHYLLIDA) *(bad accent)*

> I fear it, I promise you.

All stop and stare

ALL Ooh aargh.

BOTTOM (DAVE)

> A lion among ladies is a most dreadful thing; for there is not a more fearful wildfowl than your lion living; and we ought to look to't.

SNOUT (JO)

> Therefore, another prologue must tell he is not a lion.

BOTTOM (DAVE)

> Nay, you must name his name, and half his face must be seen through the lion's neck.

JO
TOM } *(putting their hands over Felix's mouth)* Like that?

DAVE No. Like that. *(He moves their hands over Felix's eyes)* That's better.

QUINCE (SIMON)

> Well, it shall be so.

ALL EXCEPT PHYLLIDA Beer!

They move in a line to exit and walk into Simon, who stops them

QUINCE (SIMON)

> There is another thing — we must have a wall; for Pyramus and Thisbe, did talk through the chink of a wall.

SNOUT (JO)

> You can never bring in a wall.

JO I mean, I'll check, but I doubt it.

Jo exits to the prompt corner

JO TO PUCK WITH HARNESS

STARVELING (PHYLLIDA)
> What say you, Bottom?

BOTTOM (DAVE)
> Some man or other must present Wall; let him hold his fingers thus,
> and through that cranny shall Pyramus and Thisbe whisper.

Tom demonstrates

QUINCE (SIMON)
> If that may be, then all is well. Come every mother's son, and
> rehearse your parts.

> *Phyllida exits*

> Pyramus, you begin.

> *Puck flies across from* L *to* R, *coming to rest at the top of the* R *pillar*

> When you have spoken your speech, enter into that brake; and so
> everyone according to his cue.

PHYLLIDA TO TITANIA

PUCK (JO)
> What hempen homespuns have we swaggering here
> So near the cradle of the Fairy Queen?
> What, a play toward? I'll be an auditor.
> *(She grabs a can of beer from the wings, opens it with a great spray and
> starts drinking)*

DAVE *(holding his hand out to the heavens)* Looks like rain, boys, we'd
better get on.

QUINCE (SIMON)
> Speak, Pyramus! Thisbe, stand forth!

BOTTOM (DAVE) as PYRAMUS *(with sword in hand)*
> Thisbe, the flowers of odious savours sweet.

QUINCE (SIMON)
> Odours — odours!

BOTTOM (DAVE) as PYRAMUS
>   ...odours savours sweet.
> *(He takes Thisbe in his arms)*
>   So hath thy breath,
> *(He drops on one knee holding Thisbe)*
>   my dearest Thisbe dear.
>   But hark, a voice.
> *(He drops Thisbe on the floor)*
>   Stay thou but here awhile,
>   And by and by I will to thee appear.

He exits R, *followed by a gleeful Puck*

FLUTE (TOM)
>   Must I speak now?

QUINCE (SIMON)
>   Aye, marry must you; for you must understand that he goes but to
>   see a noise that he heard, and is to come again.

TOM I'm not used to playing a woman, that's all. Unless you count the
time me and Phyllie were at this really strange party and someone
suggested——

SIMON Do it.

*Tom prepares himself, then does a girlie walk before speaking in his idea
of a woman's voice*

FLUTE (TOM) as THISBE
>   I'll meet thee, Pyramus, at Ninny's tomb.

QUINCE (SIMON)
>   "Ninus' tomb", man! — Why you must not speak that yet. That you
>   answer to Pyramus. You speak all your part at once, cues and all.
>   Pyramus, enter — your cue is past.

Bottom (Dave) enters R, *with an ass's head. Puck (Jo) flies in behind him*

BOTTOM (DAVE) as PYRAMUS
>   If I were fair, fair Thisbe, I were only thine.

Puck cues the Fairies

They run on shrieking to frighten the Mechanicals

There is a lot of smoke and Puck flies about, revelling in the chaos

In the smoke and confusion, Titania (Phyllida) swaps with her double and adopts the sleeping position

QUINCE (SIMON)

O monstrous! O strange! We are haunted! Pray, masters! Fly, masters! Help!

Quince (Simon), Snug (Felix), Flute (Tom) exit, followed by Puck (Jo) and the noisy Fairies

TOM TO PEASEBLOSSOM; SIMON TO MUSTARDSEED; FELIX TO FELIX; JO TO PUCK WITHOUT HARNESS

BOTTOM (DAVE)

I see their knavery! This is to make an ass of me, to fright me, if they could; but I will not stir from this place, do what they can. I will walk up and down here, and I will sing, that they shall hear I am not afraid.
(Singing) Feelings ... *(or other popular ballad)*

TITANIA (PHYLLIDA) *(awaking aroused)*

What angel wakes me from my flowery bed?
I pray thee, gentle mortal, sing again!

BOTTOM (DAVE)

Feelings ...

TITANIA (PHYLLIDA)

Mine ear is much enamoured of thy note.
(She starts to wrap herself around Bottom)
So is mine eye enthralled to thy shape,
And thy fair virtue's force perforce doth move me
On the first view to say, to swear, I love thee.

She caresses Bottom's legs and groin. He waggles his ears and seems uncomfortable

BOTTOM (DAVE)

Methinks, Mistress, you should have little reason for that. And yet, to say the truth, reason and love keep little company together nowadays. Nay, I can gleek upon occasion.

TITANIA (PHYLLIDA) *(becoming more sensual in her approach)*
Thou art as wise as thou art beautiful. *(Her hand on his groin)*

Peaseblossom (Tom) enters DL *and stands watching, furious at what is going on. Mustardseed (Simon) enters* R *and hovers uneasily*

DAVE *(squirming with embarrassment)* Could you not do that.
BOTTOM (DAVE)
Not so neither; but if I had wit enough to get out of this wood, I have enough to serve mine own turn.
TITANIA (PHYLLIDA)
Out of this wood do not desire to go!
DAVE *(covering his private parts, which are clearly in some distress)* I really am going to have to leave.
TITANIA (PHYLLIDA)
Thou shalt remain here, whether thou wilt or no.
(She pulls him to sit down next to her)
I am a spirit of no common rate.
And I do love thee. *(She kisses him)* Come with me.

Dave groans

I'll give thee fairies to attend on thee,

She tries to place her hand over his groin. He hits her hand lightly to stop her

I will purge thy mortal grossness so

She puts her hand back on his groin, he removes it

That thou shalt like an airy spirit go.

She makes a grand gesture with her hand as Dave changes his mind, grabs her hand and puts it back on his groin. As she continues to speak, Dave begins to writhe about

Peaseblossom! Mustardseed! Fairies, all!

She gets up. Dave follows her on all fours, his ass's nose close to her backside

MUSTARDSEED (SIMON)
   Hail, mortal!
PEASEBLOSSOM (TOM) *(cold anger)*
   Hail.
BOTH FAIRIES (SIMON and TOM) Where shall we go?
TITANIA (PHYLLIDA)
   Be kind and courteous to this gentleman.
   Pluck the wings from painted butterflies
   To fan the moonbeams from his sleeping eyes.
   Nod to him, elves, and do him courtesies.
   Come, wait upon him. Lead him to my bower.
   Tie up my lover's tongue; bring him silently.

Titania (Phyllida) exits to the prompt corner, followed by Mustardseed (Simon)

Dave moves to follow, until his way is blocked by Tom's legs. He slowly looks upwards, then stands and, as he realizes it is Tom, jerks back in alarm, then takes the ass's head off and looks at Tom, mortified

DAVE I'm sorry, mate. Acting!

Dave exits to the prompt corner, watched by a furious Tom

Music

Almost immediately Puck (Jo) enters UL to perform the Wood Nymph dance, waving a small gossamer scarf in each hand

TOM Phyllida! You two-timing cow!

Jo gamely tries to continue her dance

Phyllida, still dressed as Titania, enters L. Simon enters R, dressed as a Wood Nymph in a green gossamer poncho, with a large garland of greenery on his head. He holds both hands above his head and trails a giant green gossamer banner the width of the stage. Dave enters L, dressed as a Wood Nymph and holding another Wood Nymph costume

Dave confers with Jo, who indicates that the row must be stopped

PHYLLIDA That's rich, coming from a man who keeps his brain in his jock strap.

TOM Best place if I want you to notice it. And I suppose you were just helping Dave make his part larger?

PHYLLIDA Oh — and what were you doing with the Classics Mistress on Speech Day? Showing her your Doric Column?

TOM I told you — she wasn't the Classics Mistress.

DAVE *(running between Tom and Phyllida)* Wood Nymphs! I brought you your costume, Tom!

Tom throws it in the wings

As the row progresses, Jo runs on with an identical banner from L to R, which she lies parallel with Simon's

Phyllida (R) and Simon (L) pick up either end of the downstage banner, while Dave (R) and Tom (L) pick up either end of the upstage banner

JO Up! Up!

Jo encourages the four to raise their banners for her to walk underneath as she attempts to continue her dance. Passing under the banners c, she smiles at the audience. Phyllida and Simon lower their banner behind Jo. As she turns back upstage and steps over it, Phyllida brings the cloth up sharply between Jo's legs. Jo sinks to her knees in some pain, glaring at Phyllida

Meanwhile, Felix, complete with Oberon cloak and photocopied pages of the script with his part underlined, has been working his way through the stalls, quietly trying to persuade someone to play the next scene for him

The music ceases. Still on one knee, Puck (Jo) turns UR where a followspot is focused. So do the other Wood Nymphs, who pose expectantly. Felix is gradually getting louder as he becomes more desperate

PUCK (JO)
My Lord Oberon — I bring you news...

FELIX Listen, it's two minutes, tops — it's an easy scene.

PUCK (JO) *(still kneeling, but looking about, confused, for Oberon)*
My mistress with a monster is in love.

FELIX What, you don't read English?

JO *(turning to peer out to the house)* Felix?

Silence on stage as all the actors realize where Felix is and wonder what he is doing

FELIX *(to the cast)* Sorry, guys. Slight hold up. I'm not available for the next scene. I'm just fixing up a stand in. *(Picking on a member of the audience)* This guy ... terrific Oberon. We're looking at a major league talent here. *(To a member of the audience)* It's just for the one scene, really, I——

JO Get up on the stage, Felix.

FELIX I don't have time right now. *(He carries on trying to persuade someone to take his part)*

PHYLLIDA That's it. I'm leaving.

Phyllida throws down her end of the banner and exits

DAVE Jo, there's no-one on the other end of my banner.

JO Don't make me kill you, Dave. Go and put the lights on and get my cans. Felix...

Dave exits to the prompt corner to put on the worker lights. He returns with Jo's headset as the row continues

FELIX C'mon, ladies and gentlemen. *(Moving up on to the stage)* Gimme a break — I only want to listen to one lousy little race.

JO Race? What race?

FELIX *(realizing he's said too much)* A tiny race ... a race with ... little tiny dogs. Cute, real cute. It's nothing. *(He produces a radio and headphones. He puts the headphones on)* But it is on in a minute.

JO You've been gambling again — where'd you get the money?

FELIX *(eyeing the audience)* It was just lying there — oh God, they've announced the race.

JO Oh no you don't.

She grabs the headphones off Felix's head and moves c. *Felix goes after her, but Dave moves between them to protect her*

DAVE Don't you touch her.
JO *(hiding behind Dave)* I'm with him.
FELIX *(checking his watch, desperate)* All right. All right. I've put this evening's box-office takings on a greyhound in the Gold Ribbon Cup at Catford Dogs. *(Or local reference)*
JO *(dropping the headphones in shock)* You mean to say you've bet these people's money on a dog?

Felix grabs the headphones

SIMON This would never have happened at The National. *(Or local reference)*
FELIX *(putting the headphones on, turning the radio up)* They're going into the traps.
TOM What are the odds?
FELIX Ten to one.
DAVE Fab! So everyone in the audience could make ten times their ticket money?
FELIX That wasn't exactly the plan——

Dave, Tom and Jo advance menacingly towards him

— but it's a good plan.
SIMON Honestly, if this carries on, I shall faint.
FELIX The hare's running ...

With a loud cry, Simon faints — everyone ignores him. Felix relates the sports commentary that he's hearing in his ear, becoming more like a sports commentator as the excitement mounts

... and they're off! And away ... even break... Dal's Outing just goes ahead of Piglet Surprise and Cissy Fairfax ... that's our dog!
JO *(to the audience)* Cissy Fairfax — that's our dog.
FELIX Round the first bend, Dal's Outing goes a length clear, with Peta's Pride looking strong, but still no show from Cissy Fairfax. Come on, Cissy. Going down the back straight, Dal's Outing now leading by a length, ooh ... there's a bit of bumping — Dal's Outing and Piglet

Surprise run wide, leaving outsider Cissy Fairfax with an opening. Approaching the bend, Dal's Outing still leads with Cissy Fairfax making a valiant attempt to close the gap. Coming up towards the line, Cissy Fairfax and Dal's Outing are neck and neck together. It's very close — Dal's Outing tries to hold on, but Cissy Fairfax makes a last surge, and just forges ahead. It's Cissy Fairfax, the winner! She won! Our dog won! We won! Everyone to the bar — Jo, call an interval.

JO *(through her headset)* Ladies and gentlemen, we've going to have an interval — see you in about twenty minutes.

Tom exits R. *Dave and Jo exit to the prompt corner, both stepping over Simon without looking at him*

DAVE *(as they exit)* I've never won anything before.

JO You haven't now — you didn't buy a ticket.

FELIX *(exiting through the house; euphoric)* Go spend your money — get yourselves a drink. I can't believe I'm going to collect the winnings dressed like this!

Felix exits. As the audience leave, Simon continues to lie where he fell, then realizes that the others have gone and it's the interval. He stands and walks off, very confused

JO TO JO WITH HARNESS; DAVE TO LYSANDER; FELIX TO OBERON WITH GLITTER; PHYLLIDA TO HELENA; TOM TO DEMETRIUS; SIMON TO SIMON

INTERVAL

ACT II

Scene 1

As the audience come back to their seats, two spotlights "play" across the tabs. Dave and Jo, both dressed in their theatre "blacks", enter through the centre of the tabs. Jo is wearing her glasses again and has her headset round her neck. They stand awkwardly in front of the tabs

DAVE Do you want to tell them, or shall I?
JO You go ahead.

Dave tries to tuck his shirt in. Jo slaps his hand

Don't do that, it's horrid.
DAVE Uhm, it seems that while Cissy Fairfax was the undisputed winner, uhm...the dog has been the subject of a steward's enquiry. A dope test has unfortunately revealed that she is ...
JO ... the Ben Jonson of dog racing.
DAVE Yes, well it's not quite as simple as that, Jo. I mean, it was partly her collapsing at the finish line and ...
JO ... partly, she was the only dog to be helped off the track by the rabbit.
DAVE So you get no money.
JO Thank you, Dave.
DAVE And I don't get to play Bottom. *(He begins to weep quietly, resting his head on Jo's shoulder)*
JO *(patting his leg)* Yes, all right, pull yourself together. *(Feeling his pocket)* What is that?
DAVE My hanky.

JO Oh. Felix ... Mr Barker, would have been here to explain it to you, but after the news came through, er, he went a bit ...
DAVE ... loony. He's gone potty. Barking tonto.
JO I can only ...

There is the sound of the opening bars of "There's No Business Like Show Business" played very loudly as the tabs rise. Jo and Dave get out of the way

All the young Fairies enter in gold top hats and glitter waistcoats and line the steps down the bank. Felix makes a fabulous entrance at the top of the bank, dressed in a gold top hat and tails. As he and the Fairies begin to sing "There's No Business Like Show Business", Felix slowly descends the steps of the bank. As he treads on each one, it lights up in the great showbiz tradition. They do a complete number with Jo and Dave trying to encourage the Fairies to leave the stage

Tom enters the back of the auditorium with a pint and enjoys the spectacle enormously. At the end of the song, the Fairies exit, ushered out by Jo and Dave

Jo and Dave are both nervous about approaching Felix as he seems quite mad. Tom gets up on the stage with his pint, full of admiration for Felix

JO Felix, you're over tired. Come and lie down in your office.
FELIX Look, I may be arrested at any moment, but when I go, I'm going in style.

Felix tips his top hat in a cavalier fashion and makes a grand exit L

TOM Wasn't he great?
JO Tom, get off the stage. What are you doing drinking?

Jo and Tom exit L *after Felix. Dave exits* R

Simon enters R, *dressed in a shabby track suit and Oberon's cloak, holding a script. He furtively checks that the coast is clear*

SIMON (*declaiming with great fervour*)
     I wonder if Titania be awaked ...

Felix, minus his hat and coat, enters L and slowly advances on Simon

    (Continuing oblivious to the approaching storm)
      Then what it was that next came in her eye,
      Which she must dote on, in extremity.
      Here comes my ... *(suddenly spotting Felix)* ... messenger.

*Felix eyes Simon, then slowly opens his cloak and puts it on, with Simon
still inside it. He moves to C, dragging Simon with him*

    Jo (prompt corner) and Dave (R) hover nervously

OBERON (FELIX)
      I wonder if Titania be awaked;
      Then what it was that next came in her eye,
      Which she must dote on, in extremity.

He yanks the cloak around himself, crushing Simon

JO Dave, get him out from under there!

Simon slides down Felix's back

    Dave drags him off by the foot, R

DAVE Don't worry, Simon, you can put it on your c.v.

*Felix adjusts the Oberon cloak around himself and make a grand gesture
to the flies. The forest flies in and the Lights change*

    Dave runs back on to Jo, carrying her Puck costume

He avoids Felix who is pacing the stage, power mad

DAVE Bit of Puck.
JO Dave, he's not well. I can't ...
DAVE Go on. Give me your glasses.

*Dave helps Jo into the Puck costume, takes her glasses from her and puts on
her headset as if taking over her stage management duty. He indicates C*

In the middle. I'm watching out for you. "My mistress with a monster
is in love".

OBERON (FELIX) *(rounding on Jo)*
> Here comes my messenger.
> How now, mad spirit?

PUCK (JO) *(very nervous)*
> My mistress with a monster is in love.

Dave gives her a thumbs up and exits to the prompt corner

OBERON (FELIX)
> This falls out better than I could devise!

JO Oh good.

OBERON (FELIX)
> But hast thou yet latched the Athenian's eyes
> With the love juice, as I did bid thee do?

PUCK (JO) *(gaining confidence as she remembers the plot)*
> I took him sleeping — that is finished too;
> And the Athenian woman by his side,
> That when he waked of force she must be eyed.

DEMETRIUS (TOM) *(off)*
> Oh, Hermia...

OBERON (FELIX)
> Stand close.

FELIX Go!

Puck (Jo) runs to hide behind the banks, chased by the demented Oberon
(Felix)

A double for Hermia runs straight across the stage, L to R, chased by
Demetrius (Tom). Demetrius moves to C, dispirited by the chase

JO's DOUBLE TO PUCK

OBERON (FELIX)
> This is the same Athenian.

PUCK (JO)
> This is the woman, but not this the man.

FELIX What?

Felix goes to strike Puck (Jo) who ducks behind the steps. Oberon stays watching

Puck (Jo) sneaks away

<u>JO TO HERMIA</u>

Demetrius checks his breath, then removes a small breath freshener spray from under his toga and sprays his mouth. He pauses, then sprays his groin. After a moment it starts to sting and he doubles in pain

Hermia (Jo) enters R, rubbing her leg from the chase. Jo's double takes her place beside Oberon at the back of the steps

DEMETRIUS (TOM)
    O, why rebuke you him that loves you so?
    Lay breath so bitter on your bitter foe.
HERMIA (JO)
    Now I but chide; but I should use thee worse,
    For thou, I fear, hast given me cause to curse.
    If thou hast slain Lysander in his sleep,
    Being o'er shoes in blood, plunge in the deep,
    And kill me too.
    The sun was not so true unto the day
    As he to me. Would he have stolen away
    From sleeping Hermia?
    It cannot be but thou hast murdered him.
    So should a murderer look; so dead, so grim.
DEMETRIUS (TOM) *(sitting on the bank)*
    So should the murdered look, and so should I,
    Pierced through the heart with your stern cruelty.
    Yet you, the murderer, look as bright, as clear,
    As yonder Venus in her glimmering sphere.
HERMIA (JO) *(getting up and moving away from him)*
    What's this to my Lysander? Where is he?
    Ah, good Demetrius, wilt thou give him me?
DEMETRIUS (TOM) *(coming up behind her)*
    You spend your passion on a misprised mood.
    I am not guilty of Lysander's blood.
    Nor is he dead, for aught that I can tell.

HERMIA (JO) *(relieved, sinking back into Tom's arms)*
  I pray thee, tell me then that he is well.
DEMETRIUS (TOM)
  An if I could, what should I get therefore?
  (He gently kisses the top of Jo's head)
HERMIA (JO)
  A privilege never to see me more.
TOM I'm sorry. I shouldn't have kissed you.
HERMIA (JO)
  And from thy hated presence part I so.
  See me no more, whether he be dead or no.

She moves to exit R. *Tom grabs her arm*

TOM Jo? You're not going are you?
JO *(turning)* That's the end of my bit. I get cross with you and then I'm off. What's the matter?
TOM Nothing. It's just that I don't want to be on my own. I feel a bit down you know, Phyllie and I had that row and...

We see Phyllida in the L *wings, watching*

JO *(moving towards Tom awkwardly)* I'm sorry, it'll be all right. *(She pats his arm)*
TOM Do you really think so?
JO Oh yes. People have these little spats and ... oh ...

As she speaks, Tom turns towards her and moves in to kiss her. Jo only stops him at the last moment

  Do you mind? Firstly, I said "no snogging" and ... is it really as big as they say?...
TOM Bigger.
JO ... and secondly — I thought you were trying to get Phyllida back?
TOM I am. Sorry, no offence. Only a bit of fun. Always worth a pop.
  (He puts his arm round Jo and tickles her neck)
JO Of course. No, don't do that.
TOM Why not?
JO Well, it's quite nice and ... oh ...

Tom moves in and this time does kiss her. As he pulls away, Jo stands shocked for a moment, then slaps him hard in the face

For goodness sake, pull yourself together. There must be something in the water in St Martin's Lane. *(Or local reference)*

As Jo moves to exit R, Phyllida comes on and drags her off by the arm

Now, Phyllida...
PHYLLIDA You come here.
JO I can explain...

Phyllida and Jo exit L, there is an immediate sound of slapping and exclamations from Jo backstage. During the commotion, the Puck double slips away from her position next to Oberon

JO TO PUCK

DEMETRIUS (TOM)
There is no following her in this fierce vein.
Here therefore for a while I will remain.
So sorrow's heaviness doth heavier grow
For debt that bankrupt sleep doth sorrow owe.
(He lies down and sleeps)

Phyllida and Jo, (now dressed as Puck) are heard behind the bank

PHYLLIDA *(off)* I saw you lead him on, tart.
JO *(off)* I did not. Anyway, I thought it was over between you.
PHYLLIDA *(off)* I'm just bringing him to heel — so butt out, you poisonous little troll.
JO *(off)* Ow!

Jo is pushed into view by Phyllida, straight into the arms of Oberon, who is clearly angry

Oh ... hello?

Jo runs downstage to escape, as Oberon stands up from his hiding place

OBERON (FELIX)
>What hast thou done? Thou hast mistaken quite,
>And laid the love juice on some true love's sight.

JO Sorry.

OBERON (FELIX)
>About the wood go swifter than the wind,
>And Helena of Athens look thou find.
>All fancy-sick she is and pale of cheer
>With sighs of love, that costs the fresh blood dear.

JO Well, I'll know her then.

OBERON (FELIX)
>By some illusion see thou bring her here.
>I'll charm his eyes against she do appear.

PUCK (JO)
>I go, I go — look how I go — *(trying to fly)*
>Swifter than arrow from the Tartar's bow.
>*(She leaps in the air, trying to fly. It is unsuccessful)*

JO I forgot my wings. I'll be off then.

Jo exits to L flying rig

Oberon takes the flower from his pocket, goes to Demetrius, sits down on the bank and looks expectant. There is a pause. He indicates with his hand and the music starts. He mouths "thank you"

OBERON (FELIX)
>Flower of this purple dye,
>Hit with Cupid's archery,
>Sink in apple of his eye.
>When his love he doth espy,
>Let her shine as gloriously
>As the Venus of the sky.
>When thou wakest, if she be by,
>Beg of her for remedy.

He squeezes the flower on Demetrius' eyes. Tom stirs in his sleep and rubs his hand sensually over Felix's chest

FELIX *(slapping Tom's hand)* Get your hands off me.

There is a shout of joy, then Puck (Jo) enters, flying

JO I've really got the hang of this! I just love it now. *(She flies across L to R doing somersaults)* Now, backwards! *(She makes one backward somersault R to L but loses her momentum as she swings L)* Sorry, bit out of control with that one. Be right back. *(She tries to steady herself on the L pillar, which comes off in her hands. She grabs it in her arms, lands, looks uncertain and then stands it next to her as if that was what was supposed to happen)*

PUCK (JO)
    Captain of our fairy band,
    Helena is here at hand.
    And the youth mistook by me,
    Pleading for a lover's fee.

OBERON (FELIX)
    Stand aside. The noise they make
    Will cause Demetrius to awake.

Oberon stands as Puck is lifted up in the air. Still holding the pillar, she finds herself sitting astride it as she flies off, R. Jo drops the pillar in the R wings and clings to the top of the R pillar. Oberon goes and hides behind the banks

JO Haven't had my legs that wide in years. Settle down, I've got a bit of plot.

PUCK (JO)
    Then will two at once woo one —
    That must needs be sport alone;
    And those things do best please me
    That befall preposterously.

Puck (Jo) exits R

JO TO HERMIA WITHOUT HARNESS

Lysander (Dave) and Helena (Phyllida) enter UL

LYSANDER (DAVE)
    Why should you think that I should woo in scorn?

Scorn and derision never come in tears.
Look when I vow, I weep; and vows so born
In their nativity all truth appears.

HELENA (PHYLLIDA)
These vows are Hermia's. Will you give her o'er?

LYSANDER (DAVE)
I had no judgement when to her I swore.

HELENA (PHYLLIDA)
Nor none in my mind now you give her o'er.

LYSANDER (DAVE)
Demetrius loves her, and he loves not you.

He moves DL and lies down as if sunning himself. Oberon wakes Demetrius. Helena stands with her back to him, weeping

DEMETRIUS (TOM) *(awaking aroused)*
O Helen...

Helena leaps into his arms

... goddess, nymph, perfect, divine —
(He carries her downstage)
To what, my love, shall I compare thine eyne?
Crystal is muddy! *(Moving L)* O, how ripe in show
Thy lips — those kissing cherries, tempting grow.
O, let me kiss *(He kneels, still holding her)*
This princess of pure white, this seal of bliss!

Helena (Phyllida) rises, throws Demetrius (Tom) down and runs R. Tom is thrown forward and lands with his face in Lysander (Dave's) lap. Lysander awakes, disgusted

HELENA (PHYLLIDA)
O spite! O hell! I see you are all bent
To set against me for your merriment.

Demetrius (Tom) leaps to his feet. Lysander (Dave) leaps up next to him

Can you not hate me — as I know you do?
But you must join in souls to mock me too?

Demetrius (Tom) advances on Helena (Phyllida) with a slow, sexy walk and kneels at her feet. Lysander (Dave) copies Demetrius, but very badly, and also comes to rest on his knees by Helena's feet

> You both are rivals, and love Hermia;
> And now both rivals to mock Helena
> With your derision.

Starting from different sides, Demetrius (Tom) and Lysander (Dave) begin kissing round the hem of her skirt

> None of noble sort
> Would so offend a virgin, and extort
> A poor soul's patience, all to make you sport.

Helena (Phyllida) pulls her skirt away as both boys have reached the centre of the dress with their kissing, so they end up kissing each other full on the lips. They get to their feet as if stuck together at the lips, then pull away in mutual disgust

LYSANDER (DAVE) *(taking Demetrius DL)*
> You are unkind, Demetrius.

He mimes taking a snooker cue from the wall of the pros arch and putting chalk on it. He hands a mimed cue to Tom, who looks at him as if he is mad, then starts trying to imagine a snooker cue. Dave begins mime-playing snooker with his own cue, eyeing the table and bending over it to set up his shot

> Be not so,
> For you love Hermia — this you know I know.
> And hear: with all good will, with all my heart,
> In Hermia's love I yield you up my part.

He takes his shot and stands upright

> And yours of Helena to me bequeath,
> Whom I do love, and will do to my death.

HELENA (PHYLLIDA) *(moving to sit on the step)*
> Never did mockers waste more idle breath.

*Demetrius (Tom) moves Dave out of the way so he can get to the mimed
table*

DEMETRIUS (TOM)
    Lysander, keep thy Hermia. I will none.
    (He sets up a shot, shoots with ease and smiles)
    If e'er I loved her all that love is gone.
    My heart to her but as guestwise sojourned,

*He sets up a shot with the cue behind his back and shoots successfully.
Dave is disgusted*

    And now to Helen it is home returned
    There to remain.

*Tom hands his mimed cue back to Dave and leaps athletically over to
Helena. Lysander (Dave) puts both cues back on the wall, then unsuccess-
fully copies him, falling on his face at Helena's feet*

LYSANDER (DAVE)
    Helen, it is not so.
JO *(off)* Lysander!
DEMETRIUS (TOM)
    Look where thy love comes: yonder is thy dear.

    Hermia (Jo) enters DL, *running*

*She runs straight into Lysander's arms. He groans; while they speak,
Demetrius lies on the floor, trying to win Helena's favour*

HERMIA (JO)
    Lysander, why unkindly didst thou leave me so?
LYSANDER (DAVE)
    Why should he stay whom love doth press to go?
HERMIA (JO)
    What love could press Lysander from my side?
LYSANDER (DAVE)
    Lysander's love, that would not let him bide:
    Fair Helena, who more engilds the night

Hermia turns to look at Helena, who now has her foot on Demetrius' head as he lies squirming on the floor

> Than all yon fiery oes and eyes of light,
> Why seekest thou me? Could not this make thee know
> The hate I bare thee made me leave thee so?

Stepping on Demetrius' head, Helena gets up and moves R

HERMIA (JO)
> You speak not as you think. It cannot be.

Lysander moves towards Helena. Demetrius rises. Both men advance on Helena as she speaks; Hermia moves to sit on the stump of the broken pillar, L

HELENA (PHYLLIDA)
> Lo, she is one of this confederacy.
> Now I perceive they have conjoined all three
> To fashion this false sport in spite of me.
> *(She knocks the two mens heads together, advances on Hermia and drags her up)*
> Injurious Hermia, O, is all forgot?

JO No.

HELENA (PHYLLIDA)
> All schooldays, friendship, childhood innocence
> Will you rent our ancient love asunder,
> To join with men in scorning your poor friend?

She grabs Hermia's hair and pulls it back. Hermia sinks to the floor

> It is not friendly, 'tis not maidenly.
> Our sex, as well as I, may chide you for it,
> Though I alone do feel the injury.

She throws Hermia forward to the floor

HERMIA (JO) *(rolling over on her back with one knee up)*
> I am amazed at your passionate words.

I scorn you not; it seems that you scorn me.

Helena (Phyllida) lunges at Hermia, who puts her foot up to stop her.
Helena grabs Hermia's foot and twists her body round on the floor

HELENA (PHYLLIDA)
Have you not set Lysander, as in scorn
To follow me and praise my eyes and face?

Jo bangs the floor with her hand to get Phyllida to stop

And made your other love, Demetrius —
Who even but now did spurn me with his foot —

She drops Jo's foot on the ground. Jo collapses on her stomach as
Phyllida moves in to sit on her back. As she speaks, she grabs Jo's head
and pulls it back

To call me goddess, nymph, divine and rare,
Precious, celestial? Wherefore speaks he this
To her he hates? *(She releases Jo's head)*
JO I don't know.
HELENA (PHYLLIDA)
And wherefore doth Lysander
Deny your love, so rich within his soul,
And tender me forsooth affection
But by your setting on...

She brings her knees sharply together over Jo's back, causing her to arc
in pain

... by your consent?

She repeats the move, then rolls off exhausted

HERMIA (JO)
I understand not what you mean by this.

Helena rises. Hermia eyes her nervously, then tries to get out of her way

JO (*mouthing to the boys)* She's not well.
HELENA (PHYLLIDA) *(noticing)*

> Ay, do! Persever, counterfeit sad looks,
> Make mouths upon me when I turn my back.

Helena grabs Hermia's nose and pulls her up

> If you have any pity, grace, or manners,
> You would not make me such an argument.

Helena smacks her own hand away from Hermia's nose

> But fare ye well.
> *(She backs away towards the men)*
> 'Tis partly my own fault,
> Which death or absence soon shall remedy.

Helena backs into Lysander's arms. Hermia follows, rubbing her nose

LYSANDER (DAVE)

> Stay, gentle Helena, hear my excuse,
> My love, my life, my soul, fair Helena!

HELENA (PHYLLIDA)

> O, excellent!

Helena pushes Lysander away, into Hermia's arms, Demetrius grabs Helena from behind

HERMIA (JO) *(moving to stand in front of Lysander, she stands on his feet to speak closer to his face)*

> Sweet, do not scorn her so.

Lysander (Dave) moves towards Helena with Hermia standing on his feet

LYSANDER (DAVE)

> Helen, I love thee. By my life, I do.

DEMETRIUS (TOM)

> I love thee more than he can do.

LYSANDER (DAVE) *(pushing Hermia away to the floor)*
    If thou say so, withdraw, and prove it too.
DEMETRIUS (TOM) *(dropping Helena to the floor, turning to Lysander)*
    Quick, come.

Hermia crawls between Lysander's legs and stands in front of him. She encircles him with her arms

HERMIA (JO)
    Lysander, whereto tends all this?
LYSANDER (DAVE)
    Away, you Ethiope!
DEMETRIUS (TOM)
    No, no. He'll
    Seem to break loose, take on as he would follow,
    But yet come not.
    (He taps Lysander provocatively on the head as he crosses L*)*
    You are a tame man, go.

Lysander (Dave) breaks loose from Hermia's grip, picks her up under the arms and dumps her on the centre step

LYSANDER (DAVE)
    Hang off, thou cat, thou burr! Vile thing, let loose.
HERMIA (JO)
    Why are you grown so rude?
    What change is this? Sweet love?
LYSANDER (DAVE)
    Thy love? — out loathed medicine!
HERMIA (JO)
    Do you not jest?
HELENA (PHYLLIDA) *(sitting dejected on the floor* DR*)*
    Yes, sooth, and so do you.
LYSANDER (DAVE)
    Demetrius, I will keep my word to thee.
DEMETRIUS (TOM)
    I'll not trust your word.
LYSANDER (DAVE) *(picking Hermia up by the front of her dress)*
    What? Should I hurt her, strike her, kill her dead?

(*He drops her on her back*)
    Although I hate her, I'll not harm her so.
HERMIA (JO) (*sitting up to hug Lysander's leg*)
    What? Can you do me greater harm than hate?
    Hate me? Wherefore? O me, what news, my love?

Lysander grabs her by the hair and kneels over her as he lays her back on the ground

JO Ow!
LYSANDER (DAVE)
    Be certain. Nothing truer — 'tis no jest
    That I do hate thee and love Helena.
    (*He blows a kiss to Helena, then lies on the bank in a reverie at her beauty*)

Tom looks at the audience, then mimes "wanker"

HERMIA (JO) (*sitting up slowly*)
    O me, you juggler...
    (*rising and taking off her dress*)
    ... you canker-blossom,
    You thief of love!

Helena realizes what is happening and gets up

    What, have you come by night
    And stolen my love's heart from him?

Hermia rushes at Helena, who runs L. Demetrius blocks Hermia, picking her up and swinging her round as Helena runs up on to the banks

HELENA (PHYLLIDA)
    Have you no modesty, no maiden shame,
    No touch of bashfulness?
    Fie, fie, you counterfeit, you puppet.
HERMIA (JO)
    Puppet?

Hermia elbows Demetrius in the stomach. He collapses to his knees

Why so?

Hermia pulls Demetrius' head back by his hair. Tom worries about his hairstyle

Ay, that way goes the game.
Now I perceive that she hath made compare
Between our statures.

She throws him forwards on to the floor. He groans. She slowly walks L, rounding on Helena. Lysander stands between them, trying to look inconspicuous

She hath urged her height,
  (She jumps on to the banks and slowly advances on Helena)
    And with her personage, her tall personage,
    Her height, forsooth, she hath prevailed with him.

Lysander grabs Hermia by the legs and she falls

And are you grown so high in his esteem
Because I am so dwarfish and so low?

Hermia kicks Lysander away and advances on Helena

How low am I, thou painted maypole? Speak!

Hermia advances up the bank as Helena creeps down, until Hermia stands head and shoulders above her rival

How low am I? — I am not yet so low
But that my nails can reach unto thine eyes.

Hermia leaps at Helena, who runs L. Reaching the broken pillar, Helena turns and puts her arms up to ward Hermia off. Hermia grabs her wrists and pins her against the wall

HELENA (PHYLLIDA)
Good Hermia, do not be so bitter with me.

I evermore did love you, Hermia;
Did ever keep your counsels ...

Hermia swings her round, begins backing Helena across the stage

... never wronged you,
Save that in love unto Demetrius
I told him of your stealth unto this wood.
He followed you. For love I followed him.

Hermia grabs Helena's nose and forces her to her knees

But he hath chid me hence, and threatened me
To strike me, spurn me — nay, to kill me too.
Let me go.

*Hermia releases Helena, looks at the boys, then the audience and is
embarrassed. She wipes her hand on her t-shirt and heads back towards
the prompt corner*

HERMIA (JO)
Why, get you gone! Who is't that hinders you?
HELENA (PHYLLIDA)
A foolish heart that I leave here behind.
HERMIA (JO)
What with Lysander?
HELENA (PHYLLIDA)
With Demetrius.
LYSANDER (DAVE) *(taking Helena's arm)*
Be not afraid; she shall not harm thee, Helena.
DEMETRIUS (TOM) *(taking Helena's other arm)*
No, sir. She shall not, though you take her part.

The men help Helena to her feet

HELENA (PHYLLIDA)
O, when she is angry she is keen and shrewd.
She was a vixen when she went to school,
And though she be but little, she is fierce.
HERMIA (JO)
Little again? Nothing but low and little?

Why will you suffer her to flout me thus?
Let me come to her.

*Hermia takes a run at Helena. The boys lift Helena on to their shoulders,
out of the way. Lysander (Dave) keeps Hermia at arm's length by holding
his hand on her head*

LYSANDER (DAVE)
Get you gone, you dwarf,
You minimum of hindering knot-grass made,
You bead, you acorn.
(He pushes Hermia to the ground)

The boys drop Helena and jostle with each other

DEMETRIUS (TOM)
You are too officious
In her behalf that scorns your services.
LYSANDER (DAVE)
Follow — if thou darest — to try whose right
Of thine or mine is most in Helena.
DEMETRIUS (TOM)
Follow? Nay, I'll go with thee, cheek by ...

Dave grabs Tom's wrist and gives him a Chinese burn

... jo-OW-owl.

*Tom stares at Dave then grabs both his nipples, twisting them round until
Dave stands on his toes in pain*

DAVE Tom, that really hurt.
TOM Yeah, well, look at my wrist.

Demetrius (Tom) and Lysander (Dave) exit UL *quickly*

Hermia and Helena slowly look up. Hermia gets to her feet and moves R
towards Helena

HERMIA (JO)
> You mistress, all this coil is long of you.
> *(Offering Helena her hand)* Go not back.

HELENA (PHYLLIDA) *(rising and backing away)*
> I will not trust you, I,
> Nor longer stay in your curst company.
> Yours hands than mine are quicker for a fray.
> My legs are longer, though, to run away!

Helena exits running DL

Hermia (Jo) watches her go, turns to wearily pick up her dress, looks L

JO Bastards!

Jo exits R

<u>JO TO PUCK</u>

SCENE 2

Oberon (Felix) sweeps out from behind the banks. He stands regally C

OBERON (FELIX)
> What fools these mortals be! Come, hobgoblin Puck...

Puck (Jo) enters L

JO There wasn't time to fly. There just wasn't time. *(To the* R *wings)* Props, I'll want all those.

Felix grabs her wings and twists them

> Ouch! That's my wings.

OBERON (FELIX)
> This is thy negligence.
> *(He pulls her* C*)*
> > *Still* thou mistakest
> > Or else committest thy knaveries wilfully.

PUCK (JO)
  Believe me, King of Shadows, I mistook.

Oberon releases her wings

  Did not you tell me I should know the man
  By the Athenian garments he had on?
  (Weeping, she moves to stand with her head against the R *pillar)* You
  did. You said he'd have Athenian garments on and I went into the woods
  and I ... *(she makes a raspberry sound to demonstrate the squirt from the*
  flower) ... in his eye. I didn't know it was the wrong one...
OBERON (FELIX) *(sitting on the bank, beckoning to Puck)*
  Hie Robin ...
PUCK (JO) Hi.

Oberon beckons her over again. She goes, still snivelling

  Well I didn't know they both had the same frock on — you should have
  been more specific. *(She sits on Oberon's knee)*
OBERON (FELIX) *(putting a glittery blindfold over Puck's eyes)*
  ...overcast the night.
  And lead these testy rivals so astray
  As one come not within another's way.

Oberon lowers the blindfold, Puck holds it with wonder as he hands her
a flower from his cloak

  Then crush this herb into Lysander's eye —
  When they next wake, all this derision
  Shall seem a dream and fruitless vision,

Jo starts looking at her watch to get Oberon to hurry up with his speech

  Whiles I in this affair do thee employ
  I'll to my Queen and beg her Indian boy,
  And then I will her charmed eye release
  From monster's view, and all things shall be peace.
PUCK (JO) *(showing Oberon the time)*
  My fairy lord, this must be done with haste,
  For night's swift dragons cut the clouds full fast.

JO *(getting up; to the audience)* And basically there's a very long speech, here, ladies and gentlemen, and all the spirits have gone to bed ...

As she talks, Oberon continues speaking softly

... give me strength.
OBERON (FELIX)
>   I with the morning's love have oft made sport,
>   And like a forester the groves may tread
>   Even till the Eastern gate all fiery red
>   Opening on Neptune with fair blessed beams
>   Turns into yellow gold, his salt green streams.
>   But notwithstanding, haste, make no delay;
>   We may effect this business yet 'ere day.

Oberon (Felix) exits

JO *(running under Oberon's speech)* You know what I'm saying? We must press on... you've no idea what the overtime rate is for a followspot operator... Fairies! Flowers, please!

Several small Fairies run on with paper flowers

Jo takes some and the Fairies move down into the house to hand them out to the audience

If you could give these out. It's just we're supposed to be in the deep forest and the show's running late. Normally this is a very expensive technical trick, but for the purposes of this evening, we're relying on Dave's imagination and a large Pritt Stick.

Jo goes into the house to hand some flowers out. She ad libs about the audience, theatre, etc.

The Fairies exit when they finish

(Getting back on stage) For those of you upstairs ... sorry. But it looks fabulous, honestly. An entire forest has grown up — it's very much as though Alan Titchmarsh has been through with two ton of manure. *(Or other gardening reference)* Now keep them nice and still. We want the

lovers to get lost, not go psychotic. There. Are you ready? Here we go. *(Pointing at the Lights)* Lighting cue thirty-five — go!

The Lights change

Demetrius (Tom) and Lysander (Dave) appear either side of the auditorium, wearing blindfolds. They are each accompanied by a Fairy

Jo holds either end of her blindfold above her head and brings it down slowly to dim the lights

PUCK (JO)
>Up and down, up and down,
>I will lead them up and down.
>I am feared in field and town.
>Goblin, lead them up and down.

During the following, Puck (Jo) turns and exits through the R loggia, looking back at what she has done

JO TO HERMIA

Lysander (Dave) led by the Fairy, climbs L steps to the stage

LYSANDER (DAVE)
>He goes before me, and still dares me on;
>When I come where he calls, then he is gone.
>The villain is much lighter-heeled than I.
>I followed fast, but faster did he fly.
>That fallen am I in dark uneven way,
>And here will rest me.

Lysander (Dave) lies down to sleep on the bank and the Fairy makes him comfortable. Meanwhile, Demetrius (Tom) led by the second Fairy, climbs the R steps to the stage

Helena (Phyllida) enters the L stalls. Hermia (Jo) enters the R stalls. Both wear blindfolds

The first Fairy goes to fetch Helena (Phyllida)

DEMETRIUS (TOM)
>Nay, then thou mockest me.
>Now, go thy way. Faintness constraineth me

To measure out my length on this cold bed.

Demetrius (Tom) lies down to sleep on the bank and the Fairy makes him comfortable

Helena (Phyllida), led by the Fairy, climbs the L *steps to the stage. The second Fairy goes to fetch Hermia (Jo)*

HELENA (PHYLLIDA)
O weary night! O long and tedious night.
Sleep, that sometimes shuts up sorrow's eye,
Steal me awhile from mine own company.

She lies down to sleep next to Demetrius (Tom). He makes a move towards her, but she moves away. He whispers something to her and takes her hand. She doesn't resist. The Fairy makes her comfortable then crouches on the bank

Hermia (Jo), led by the Fairy, climbs the R *steps to the stage*

HERMIA (JO)
Never so weary, never so in woe
I can no further crawl, no further go.
Here will I rest me till the break of day,
Heavens shield Lysander, if they mean a fray.

She lies down to sleep next to Lysander (Dave). He puts his arm around her and she moves close. The Fairy makes her comfortable and then crouches on the bank. A mist rises up to shroud the four lovers as the bank revolves

PUCK (JO) *(voice over)*
On the ground
Sleep sound.
I'll apply
To your eye,
Gentle lover, remedy.
When thou wakest,
Thou takest
True delight
In the sight

Of thy former lady's eye.
The man shall have his mare again, and all shall be well.

PHYLLIDA TO TITANIA; DAVE TO BOTTOM; TOM TO PEASE-
BLOSSOM; JO TO PUCK WITH HARNESS

SCENE 3

Loud Mendelssohn music

*Mustardseed (Simon) enters to do his Isadora Duncan dance, complete
with confetti. As he dances, rag doll Fairies appear from the flies. After
a short while, we hear a police siren and Felix, dressed as Oberon, runs
across the stage*

FELIX Simon! Quick! Hide me. They've found out about the money
and they've come to get me!
SIMON Would that it were so. Listen ...

The siren fades away

... they're going down to *The Dog and Trumpet. (Or local reference)*
Apparently there's been some sort of riot.
FELIX *(pulling himself together)* Right. Aha. *(He clears his throat)*
Actors!

*Felix exits R as Dave enters from around the back of the steps, dressed
as Bottom, carrying the ass's head*

DAVE Everything all right?

*Simon and Dave sit on the steps. The music still plays softly under the
scene*

SIMON Felix! He is ruining the show. Stealing scenes, getting all the
attention, I haven't seen a performance this big since ... Jane Seymour
played the Duchess of Windsor.
DAVE But everyone is saying Felix is surprisingly good.
SIMON Green room chit chat.

DAVE Mr Mackenzie seems to be coming round.

SIMON This is a subtle piece and there's no subtlety to his performance, no light, no shade. I think you could be subtle, Dave.

DAVE I could?

SIMON Can you keep a secret, Dave?

DAVE No.

SIMON You know the casting director who's in tonight?

DAVE Yes. Hello!

Dave waves to the man. Simon pulls him away

SIMON He is actually here to consider me for a rather large part in a new film. If we were to get rid of Felix, I could do Oberon — on my head frankly — and you could take over his other parts. You might even catch Mr Chalmers' eye yourself.

DAVE Why would I want to do that?

SIMON You can't be a stagehand all your life. Always doing the donkey work.

DAVE Very good.

SIMON What?

DAVE *(indicating the ass's head)* Donkey work.

He punches Simon on the arm in a friendly way, causing Simon to wince in pain

SIMON Yes, yes of course.

The fairy music swells until it is very loud indeed. Dave and Simon remain on stage for the next scene

SCENE 4

Titania (Phyllida) and Peaseblossom (Tom) enter R

Titania motions for Simon (Mustardseed) to get out of the way. Dave moves DL *and puts Bottom's head on. Tom takes a keen interest in how Phyllida plays this scene, the two of them are on their way to an inevitable reconciliation*

TITANIA (PHYLLIDA)
>Come, sit thee ...
>*(Unable to be heard over the music, she indicates to "cut")*
>Come, sit thee down upon this flowery bed

Bottom doesn't want to go, but is pushed from behind by Peaseblossom (Tom) and sits on the steps with Titania. Peaseblossom and Mustardseed stand above them

>While I thy amiable cheeks do coy,
>And stick muskroses in thy sleek, smooth head,
>And kiss thy fair large ears, my gentle joy.

DAVE Oh God, it's going to start again.

BOTTOM (DAVE)
>Where's Peaseblossom?

PEASEBLOSSOM (TOM) *(with menace)* Ready.

BOTTOM (DAVE)
>Scratch my head, Peaseblossom. Where's Monsieur Mustardseed?

MUSTARDSEED (SIMON)
>What's your will?

BOTTOM (DAVE)
>Help to scratch. I must to the barber's, Monsieur, for methinks I am marvellous hairy about the face. And I am such a tender ass, if my hair do but tickle me, I must scratch.

TITANIA (PHYLLIDA) *(beginning to discreetly stroke Tom's leg)*
>Say, sweet love, what thou desirest to eat.

BOTTOM (DAVE)
>Methinks I have a great desire to a bottle of hay. Good hay, sweet hay hath no fellow.

Tom is getting turned on by Phyllida. Simon is appalled

TITANIA (PHYLLIDA)
>I have a venturous fairy that shall seek
>The squirrel's hoard, and fetch thee new nuts.

Tom is now almost unable to hold down the skirt of his tutu. He is clearly trying to think about something other than what Phyllida is doing to him and the effect it is having

BOTTOM (DAVE)

> I had rather have a handful or two of dried pease. But I pray you let none of your people stir me. I have an exposition of sleep come upon me.

TITANIA (PHYLLIDA)

> Sleep thou, and I will wind thee in my arms.
> Fairies be gone, and be all ways away.

Peaseblossom (Tom) exits L in some distress and with some difficulty in walking. Mustardseed (Simon) exits R

> So doth the woodbine the sweet honeysuckle
> Gently entwist; the female ivy so
> Enrings the barky fingers of the elm.
> O, how I love thee! How I dote on thee!

Titania (Phyllida) and Bottom (Dave) sleep on the steps

TOM TO DEMETRIUS (RETURNS TO SLEEP ON THE BANK); SIMON TO THESEUS

Puck (Jo) enters flying from R, lands on the L side of the steps. Oberon (Felix) enters R with Changeling Child dressed in a miniature version of his cloak

OBERON (FELIX)

> Welcome, good Robin. Seest thou this sweet sight?
> *(He sends Child off)*

The Changeling Child exits

> Her dotage now I do begin to pity.
> For, meeting her of late behind the wood
> Seeking sweet favours for this hateful fool,
> I did upbraid her and fall out with her.
> *(He sits beside Titania)*
> When I had at my pleasure taunted her,
> And she in mild terms begged my patience,
> I then did ask of her her changeling child,
> Which straight she gave me.

And now I have the boy I will undo
This hateful imperfection of her eyes.
And, gentle Puck, take this transformed scalp
From off the head of this Athenian swain,
That, he awaking think no more
Of this night's accidents
But as the fierce vexation of a dream.
But first I will release the Fairy Queen.
(To Titania) Be as thou wast wont to be;
See as thou wast wont to see.
Now, my Titania, wake you!

TITANIA (PHYLLIDA) *(waking)*
My Oberon, what visions have I seen!
Methought I was enamoured of an ass.

OBERON (FELIX)
There lies your love.

TITANIA (PHYLLIDA) *(seeing the ass's head, quickly getting up)*
How came these things to pass?
O, how mine eyes do loathe his visage now!

OBERON (FELIX)
Robin, take off his head.

PUCK (JO) *(to Bottom, removing the head)*
Now when thou wakest with thine own fool's eyes peep.

Puck flies slowly L, coming to a halt at the tab line. She speaks as Oberon is just about to kiss Titania

Fairy king, attend, and mark:
I do hear the morning lark.

Puck (Jo) exits L

OBERON (FELIX)
Then, my Queen, in silence sad,
Trip we after night's shade.
We the globe can compass soon,
Swifter than the wandering moon.

TITANIA (PHYLLIDA)
Come, my lord, and in our flight
Tell me how it came this night

That I sleeping here was found
With this mortal on the ground.

Titania (Phyllida) exits with Oberon (Felix) R

FELIX TO EGEUS; PHYLLIDA TO HELENA (RETURNS TO SLEEP-
ING ON THE BANK)

BOTTOM (DAVE) *(waking)*
I have had a most rare vision. I have had a dream past the wit of man
to say what dream it was.

Bottom (Dave) exits L

DAVE TO LYSANDER (RETURNS TO SLEEPING ON THE BANK)

Jo enters L, *pursued by Simon dressed as Theseus*

SIMON Oh, Jo. Did you sort my wage slip?
JO Later. *(Going to the prompt corner, shouting)* So, who am I now?

Jo exits

JO TO HERMIA (RETURNS TO SLEEPING ON THE BANK)

SIMON Techies! They think the theatre couldn't run without them. *(He
realizes he has the stage to himself)* Ladies and gentlemen, Mr
Chalmers, I am pleased to give you — Theseus' speech, Act four, Scene
one. Imagine, if you will, the hunting ground at twilight, with powerful
dogs at bay. *(He moves* R *and clears his throat noisily)* I wear green.
THESEUS (SIMON) *(trying to make up for any lost ground with the
Casting Director, his performance soars over the top)*
Go, one of you; find out the forester
For now our observation is performed.
And since we have the vaward of the day,
My love shall hear the music of my hounds.
Uncouple in the western valley; let them go.

*The steps revolve as Theseus (Simon) slowly climbs to the top, as if on a
mountain. The lovers are revealed asleep*

> Dispatch, I say, and find the forester
> We will, fair queen, up to the mountain's top,
> And mark the musical confusion
> Of hounds and echo in conjunction.
>   But soft, what nymphs are these?

There is a great commotion as Egeus (Felix) enters UR *and climbs the steps to join Theseus (Simon). Felix is making the most of his part and annoying Simon*

EGEUS (FELIX)
> My lord, this is my daughter here asleep,
> And this Lysander; this Demetrius is,
> This Helena —
> I wonder of their being here together.

THESEUS (SIMON) *(trying to block Felix)*
> But speak, Egeus: is not this the day
> That Hermia should give answer of her choice?

EGEUS (FELIX) *(over-acting like mad)*
> It is, my lord.

THESEUS (SIMON)
> Go bid the huntsmen wake them with their horns.

Extremely loud horns sound; the lovers stir. Jo leaps up

JO What? What happened? Fly cue four, go and, or, don't ... I'm nearly ready ...

Dave pulls Jo back to the bank. The lovers slowly sit up. Felix's performance is so big now, that Simon has to battle to keep up with him

THESEUS (SIMON)
> Good morrow, friends — Saint Valentine is past!
> Begin these woodbirds but to couple now?
> I pray you all, stand up.
> I know you two are rival enemies.
> How comes this gentle concord in the world?

LYSANDER (DAVE)
> My lord, I shall reply amazedly,

Half sleep, half waking. But as yet, I swear,
I cannot truly say how I came here.
Now I do bethink me:
I came with Hermia hither. *(He kisses her)* Our intent
Was to be gone from Athens where we might
Without the peril of the Athenian law ...

Felix whacks Simon out of the way. He disappears backwards down the
steps

EGEUS (FELIX)
Enough, enough — my lord, you have enough!
I beg the law, the law upon his head.
They would have stolen away, they would, Demetrius,
Thereby to have defeated you and me.
DEMETRIUS (TOM)
But, my good lord — I wot not by what power,
But by some power it is — my love to Hermia,
Melted as the snow.
And all the faith, the virtue of my heart,
The object and the pleasure of mine eye,
Is only Helena.
PHYLLIDA Oh Tom!

Simon reappears and launches himself at Felix, making him collapse on
the top step

THESEUS (SIMON) *(lying on Felix to hold him down)*
Egeus, I will overbear your will;
For in the temple by and by with us
These couples shall be eternally knit.
Away with us to Athens. Three and three,
We'll hold a feast in great solemnity.

The lovers exit R

Theseus (Simon) and Egeus (Felix) battle it out. Theseus (Simon) disap-
pears down the steps

SIMON TO QUINCE

As the others are going off, Jo rushes from R to the prompt corner

JO Stand by for curtain call. Stand by tabs. Stand by cues ninety to ninety-four. Ninety — go! Stand by flies.

Dave enters R

(Grabbing her headset and putting it on) Kettle on in the green room. Max, Miss Brewster's car. Let's go, go, go. Tabs in.

Jo exits to L flying rig

FELIX Jo! What are you doing? We haven't finished yet. We haven't done the whole play, with Pyramus and Thisbe. You're on again.

Felix follows Jo

Dave signals for tabs in

They fly in too far and knock Tom over as he enters DR

JO *(off)* I can't be. I am!

The tabs are still coming in

(Off) Tabs out! Out, out, out!

The tabs fly out again and appear to pull Dave up with them. Felix runs from L to R as Jo flies in on the harness, still dressed as Hermia and wearing the headset

FELIX Jo! Phyllida, Simon, Tom!

Phyllida enters R. She crosses DL. Simon enters UL and moves downstage. He hasn't had time to finish changing and looks absurd

PHYLLIDA Wrong costume!

SIMON Wrong scene!

Jo flies backwards

TOM Wrong way!
FELIX Stop her, Dave!

Jo flies into the middle of the stage. Dave grabs her

DAVE Is your harness too tight?
JO Of course it's too bloody tight. This part's normally played by a twelve year old boy. I've been chafed from here to there and never a stop for Vaseline. My inner thigh looks like two pound of pig's liver. I don't know whether I'm coming or going. I've been cueing the lighting, helping with the quick changes, mopping up after Mr Mackenzie and hired a solicitor to get the rest of the cast out of prison. I've played Hermia, Puck, Snout — been beaten up as all of them. I've been felt up by a gym teacher, abused by an overweight fraudulent fairy king, looked down on by a tight-assed, over-sexed, undertalented nympho-maniac and the Coliseum *(local reference)* came round to see if they could borrow some light bulbs.
SIMON Are you saying you didn't sort my wages slip?

Jo screams and tries to kick Simon. Felix reaches up to take her by the ankle

JO I'm going to kill him — I'll kill him.
FELIX Whoa, easy, girl, steady, steady.

Felix takes Jo off L

JO *(weeping)* And I'm short.

Jo exits with Felix

Long pause

PHYLLIDA Well — there's a display.

An awkward pause

DAVE Jo, would you like us to ... *(He looks to the wings and realizes Jo isn't ready)* ... er, no.

Pause

SIMON *(looking at his watch)* Well, I think there's still time. *(To the Casting Director)* Fancy a ... *(He mimes a drink)*
PHYLLIDA *(crossing R to Tom)* Come along, Tom.

Phyllida and Tom start to exit

My conscience is clear. We've done all we can.

Simon exits L

DAVE Where are you going? You can't go. We haven't done Bottom's play at the end. It's the most famous bit. Mr Mackenzie's been helping me with my lines. I'm Bottom!
TOM Sorry, mate.

Tom exits R with Phyllida

DAVE No, please! Don't go.

Dave tries to stop them and then reappears desperately disappointed and looks to the house

Ladies and gentlemen, don't let them go. We've got to finish the play. You want to see my Bottom, don't you? Then shout out "Show us your Bottom." One, two, three ... *(He ad libs with the audience)*

Simon enters L dressed as Quince

SIMON Look Dave, it's all very well, but this is the one part of the show where you need more than six people. We've gone as far as we can go.

Simon exits L. Felix leads Jo on L. She is exhausted

DAVE No we haven't. Look, here's Jo. Jo's back! Jo's back. You see?
JO I can't do any more.

DAVE You won't have to. We'll get help. Help ... *(He has an idea. He turns slowly to look at the audience)*

Jo sits on the step

Felix exits R, brings Tom and Phyllida on, then exits L

Tom and Phyllida canoodle on the R step

Simon enters and stands DL

DAVE Fairies! Props.

Some Fairies enter R with the "HISP" props basket. They open it and Dave removes a box of torches. Two other Fairies enter L with some large boards with the audience's Shakespeare lines on, which they hand to Simon so that the writing is obscured from the audience

NB. To Dave: guideline script—ad lib around the information, according to audience reaction

DAVE Now, we need some moonlight upstairs ... Tom, could you take the torches upstairs ...
TOM *(engrossed with Phyllida)* Why?
DAVE ... to the ladies!

Tom instantly grabs the box and runs up the centre aisle to the balcony. Phyllida sits down next to Jo, but ignores her. Dave takes some red and green paper "toadstool" hats from the basket

You two fairies hand out the toadstool hats over here. *(He hands them red hats and indicates the right-hand side of the stalls)* You lot, you're the red team.

Two Fairies go into stalls and hand out red toadstool hats

Hats on your heads, come on. Upstairs? We need a bit of dog barking. Can you do a little bit of "Woof, woof, woof"?

The audience respond

That's rather too restrained. Bit more Doberman, bit less Chihuahua.

The audience respond

Felix enters L with a cup of water which he hands to Jo. He sits next to her

Fine, well done, etc. Now red team, all got your hats on? The balcony have to improvise their bit, you've got it easy — I'm going to give you your line — "It is the wittiest partition that ever I heard discourse." OK, let's hear you then. *(He tries to get them to speak)*

Simon looks disgusted

Simon, give them a hand.

Simon holds up the appropriate board with the words on

Come on, in your best Shakespeare ... go! *(He gets the red team to speak)* Right, you two fairies, you give out the green hats over here ...

He hands them green "toadstool" hats and indicates left-hand side of the stalls. The Fairies go to hand out hats

... now we need some kissing ...

FELIX *(jumping up)* I'll take care of this. You all know how to kiss don't you? You just pucker up and blow. *(He ad libs to get the audience to make kissing sounds en masse, then returns to sit next to Jo)*

DAVE Green team ready? *(Possible ad lib re wearing of hats)* It was funny making the red team speak, wasn't it? *(Pause)* Here's your line.

Simon holds up the appropriate board

"I am aweary of this moon would he would change."

Audience practice

SIMON Diction, please!

DAVE So, we've got the dogs upstairs, we need something big from downstairs. I know! We need a lion's roar — but a really big one. Got it — a Mexican lion's roar.

SIMON Sorry, Dave ... a Mexican lion's roar?

TOM *(coming down the centre aisle)* Well, obviously, that's like a Mexican wave, but you roar as you go. Mexico '86, Maradonna, hand of God. *(He jumps on stage)* My department, I think. Right, you lot go and strip down to your gym knickers and leave this to me. Simon, give us a hand.

Phyllida gives him a dirty look

Don't look like that, Phyllie, it's going to be great.

Phyllida, Jo, Felix and Dave exit

JO TO WALL (SNOUT) WITHOUT HARNESS; DAVE TO PYRAMUS (BOTTOM); PHYLLIDA TO MOONLIGHT (STARVELING); FELIX TO LION (SNUG)

Now, a Mexican lion's roar. It works like this: it's started by the people on this end of each row ... *(he indicates to his left)* ... so if you're on this end of a row you start it off. You stand up, put your arms in the air and roar. Simon and I will show you what we mean.

They stand next to each other with their backs to the audience. Simon raises his arms in the air and roars, followed by Tom

No applause, please, because you're doing it next. In the balcony, you put your arms up in the air and roar, but downstairs you stand up, put your arms up in the air and roar. Simon will show you what I mean. Imagine I'm the seat ...

Simon stands very seriously as Tom puts one arm in the air and one straight out to form a "theatre seat" which Simon crouches on as if sitting, he gives a long look at the audience, then stands, raises his arms and roars elegantly. As he does so, Tom brings the "seat" arm up so when Simon goes to sit down again, he falls to the floor

These seats tip up! Well worth knowing. So, as the person on your right does that, so you do it in turn, then the next person and the next person and so on and so on, all the way across the stalls ending up with ... you!

(He points to his right at someone on the end of a row in the stalls) Now this isn't an ordinary roar, oh no ... it starts as a big roar and ends up as an enormous roar. So we require a climax from this gentleman/lady over here. *(Ad lib comment re person's air of confidence, etc.)* So start over here, hands in the air, all the way across, climax at the end. There's a signal, a cue that you have to watch out for, which Simon is going to show us. Simon.

He demonstrates

So when you see that, you go into the Mexican Lion's Roar, OK? Now I want to see everybody doing this. I don't want to have to single people out ... but I will. All right? Get your programmes and coats off your laps and get ready to do the Mexican Lion's Roar. Watch Simon for the signal and then roar all the way across. Simon!

Simon prepares himself, then gives the signal and Tom encourages the audience across

Very good. *(He comments on the audience's performance, who didn't join in, etc.)* What we'll do now is rehearse all the parts that you play, so that you will have had more rehearsal than we have.
SIMON Red team!

Simon holds up a board for audience. They respond

Kissing!

Audience respond

Dog barking!

Audience respond

TOM Now people with torches.
SIMON Moonlight!
TOM Torches on. Right, turn them off — save the batteries, you may need them later. Now — green team.
SIMON Green Team!

Simon holds up a board. The audience respond. Tom comments on the green team versus the red team performance

TOM Now we're not going to practice the Lion's roar — yes, I know you're disappointed, but let's show some consideration for this gentle-man/lady over here, who's going to have to produce another great climax for us shortly — we don't want him/her to peak too soon. So, keep your eyes on Simon and he'll tell you what to do. Ready? On your marks ... stand by ... and ... GO!

Tom blows a PE whistle, moves L to catch his Thisbe costume which is thrown at him. The tabs come in. Simon moves c to take charge. NB. The Pyramus and Thisbe play is performed at great pace

QUINCE (SIMON) as PROLOGUE
      The actors are at hand.

Bottom as Pyramus (Dave) and Snug as Lion (Felix) enter R, running. Snout as Wall (Jo), Starveling as Moonshine (Phyllida) enter L, running and stand either side of Quince (Simon). Tom stands between Jo and Phyllida

      And they by their show
      You shall know all that you are like to know.

Everyone bows. Snout (Jo) as Wall takes c

Snug (Felix) as Lion and Bottom (Dave) as Pyramus exit R. Starveling (Phyllida) as Moon and Tom exit L

Tom puts his Thisbe costume on

SIMON Easy everyone, I'm in charge. *(He positions himself with his boards L)*
SNOUT (JO) as WALL
      In this same interlude it doth befall
      That I — one Snout by name — present a wall.
      And this the cranny, right and sinister,
      Through which the fearful lovers are to whisper.
JO Was that OK?

Simon holds up the board for the red team

RED TEAM
　　It is the wittiest partition that ever I heard discourse.
JO That's very kind — thanks very much.

　Bottom (Dave) as Pyramus enters R

BOTTOM (DAVE) as PYRAMUS
　　O wall, O sweet, O lovely wall,
JO They know I'm a wall.
DAVE Righto.
BOTTOM (DAVE) as PYRAMUS
　　... Show me thy chink to blink through with mine eyne.

Wall holds up a saucepan with a hole in the bottom

　　But what see I? No Thisbe do I see.
　　(To Wall) Curst be thy stones for thus deceiving me.

　Flute (Tom) as Thisbe enters L

FLUTE (TOM) as THISBE
　　O Wall, full often has thou heard my moans
　　For parting my fair Pyramus and me.
　　My cherry lips have often kissed thy stones,
　　Thy stones with lime and hair knit up in thee.
　(He gives Jo a very gentle kiss on the forehead and a thumbs up)
BOTTOM (DAVE) AS PYRAMUS
　　I see a voice. Now will I to the chink
　　To spy and I can hear my Thisbe's face.
　　Thisbe!
FLUTE (TOM) as THISBE
　　My love! Thou art my love, I think?
BOTTOM (DAVE) as PYRAMUS
　　O, kiss me through the hole of this vile wall!
SIMON Kisses!

The audience make kissing noises

FLUTE (TOM) as THISBE
I kiss the wall's hole, not your lips at all.
BOTTOM (DAVE) as PYRAMUS
Wilt thou at Ninny's tomb meet me straightway?
FLUTE (TOM) as THISBE
Tide life, tide death, I come without delay.

Pyramus (Dave) exits R *and Thisbe (Tom)* L

SNOUT (JO) as WALL
Thus have I, Wall, my part discharged so;
And being done, thus Wall away doth go.
(He takes a small bow and moves L*)*
JO I'm going to go and watch upstairs. *(She takes the Wall costume off and runs up the centre aisle to the balcony, where she will encourage the audience to play their part)*

Snug (Felix) as Lion enters R

SNUG (FELIX) as LION
You, ladies — you whose gentle hearts do fear
The smallest monstrous mouse that creeps on floor
May now, perchance, both quake and tremble here,
When Lion rough in wildest rage doth roar.
SIMON Roar!

The audience do the Mexican roar

Starveling (Phyllida) as Moonshine enters L *to* C, *extremely fed up with the entire proceedings*

STARVELING (PHYLLIDA) as MOONSHINE
This lanthorn doth the horned moon present;
I myself the man i'th'moon do seem to be.
SIMON Green team!
GREEN TEAM
I am aweary of this moon. Would he would change.
PHYLLIDA I've had nothing but insults all evening.

STARVELING (PHYLLIDA) as MOONSHINE
>All that I have to say is to tell you that the lantern is the moon, I the
>man i'th'moon, this thorn bush my thorn bush and this dog my dog.

SIMON Woof!

The audience bark

Flute (Tom) as Thisbe enters L, *running to* C

FLUTE (TOM) as THISBE
>This is old Ninny's tomb. Where is my love?

*Snug (Felix) as Lion pounces on Thisbe from behind and grabs her
mantle. Thisbe (Tom) runs off* L. *Lion (Felix) mauls Thisbe's mantle,
drops it and exits* L. *Bottom (Dave) as Pyramus enters* R, *lit only by a
single followspot*

SIMON Moonlight! *(To the wings)* Less light, less light!

Black-out. The audience put torches on

BOTTOM (DAVE) as PYRAMUS
>I thank thee, Moon, for shining now so bright;

DAVE And for keeping still. On me.

BOTTOM (DAVE) as PYRAMUS
>I thank thee, Moon, for shining now so bright;
>For by thy golden glittering beams
>I trust to take of truest Thisbe sight.
>Eyes, do you see? —
>How can it be?
>O dainty duck, O dear!
>Thy mantle good —
>What, stained with blood!
>Approach, ye Furies fell.
>Come tears, confound;
>Out sword, and wound
>The pap of Pyramus.
>Thus die I — thus, thus, thus.
>*(He stabs himself)* Now am I dead,
>Now am I fled;

My soul is in the sky.
Tongue, lose thy light;
Moon, take thy flight;

Starveling (Phyllida) as Moonshine exits L

JO Torches off!
BOTTOM (DAVE) as PYRAMUS
Now die, die, die, die, die.
(He dies)

Flute (Tom) as Thisbe enters L

A followspot still focuses on Pyramus (Dave)

FLUTE (TOM) as THISBE
Asleep, my love?
What, dead, my dove?
TOM *(ducking down into followspot light)* Yeah, on me. *(He encourages followspot to move up with him)* Thank you.
FLUTE (TOM) as THISBE
Tongue, not a word!
Come, trusty sword,

He pulls the sword from Pyramus, who winces and starts up

TOM Sorry.
FLUTE (TOM) as THISBE
Come blade, my breast imbrue.
(He stabs himself) And farewell friends.
Thus Thisbe ends.
SIMON *(holding up a board with "adieu, adieu, adieu" on it)* Everybody!
AUDIENCE Adieu, adieu, adieu!

Thisbe dies

The Lights come up as Dave and Tom congratulate the audience. Simon moves to the top of the steps and opens the portals. A single spot lights Simon and a fine mist rises

Jo runs back down from the balcony. Tom and Dave exit

SIMON
> The iron tongue of midnight hath told twelve.
> Lovers to bed; 'tis almost fairy time.
> Sweet friends, to bed.

Simon closes the portals. Black-out

Simon exits in the darkness

The Lights come up

> *Jo enters down the centre aisle, dressed as Snout. Dave enters to tidy up the props from the "play", highly over excited*

JO Dave, Dave! *(She climbs on stage and stands on the revolve)*
DAVE You did it! We did it! I mean there was a couple of shaky moments back there, but we soldiered on to the end. You carry on, I'm just going to set up for tomorrow.
JO Dave!
DAVE Please, I must get on. You know how everybody always goes for a drink after the show? Well, they never wait for me and I really want to be there tonight. One of the gang ... just for tonight. *(He moves R, and collects the revolve control box)*
JO Yeah, no ... I just thought, maybe you'd like to have a drink with me?
DAVE *(holding the revolve control)* What just the two of us?
JO If you like.
DAVE All right.

Jo puts her arms up to him and he moves towards her, but presses the revolve button at the same time: Jo whirls away from him

> *Felix enters R with a whoop of joy and lifts Jo off the revolve*

FELIX Marry me?
JO What?
FELIX You know Mr Chalmers? The casting director? He's decided that I, Felix Barker, will be perfect in the lead role of his new film. I shall be rich! I shall think *(clicking his fingers)* "that!" of paying The Albery *(or local reference)* back.

JO Oh Felix.

DAVE I thought Simon was up for that part?

FELIX That's showbiz.

JO How's he taking it?

Simon appears in the wings and drapes himself dramatically against the L pros arch, totally dejected

FELIX Not great.

JO *(looking R)* Phyllida, must you do that in the wings?

Phyllida appears R, dragging a besotted Tom

PHYLLIDA Jo, sorry love. You'll be pleased to know that Tom and I have reached an understanding.

DAVE You two back together again, then?

PHYLLIDA I couldn't resist that smooth tongue of his.

DAVE Talked you into it, did he?

PHYLLIDA No.

Simon, Felix, Tom, Phyllida and Dave stand in a semi circle around Jo, as the Lights dim. Jo is picked up in a soft spot

JO   If we shadows have offended,
             Think but this, and all is mended:
             That you have but slumbered here
             While these visions did appear.
             And this weak and idle theme,
             No more yielding but a dream,
             Gentles, do not reprehend
             If you pardon, we will mend.
             So, goodnight unto you all.
             Give me your hands if we be friends,
             And Robin shall restore amends.

CURTAIN

FURNITURE AND PROPERTY LIST

ACT I

SCENE 1

On stage: Grassy banks with steps

Off stage: Prompt book (**Jo**)
Phone and lead (**Jo**)
Tool box with tools (**Dave**)
Pencil (**Jo**)
Chair (**Dave**)
Bag containing medicaments and towel (**Simon**)
Open packet of crisps (**Felix**)
Script (**Jo**)
Pile of scripts   (**Jo**)
Smoke machine (**Dave**)

Personal: **Jo**: wrist-watch, headphones, glasses, (all used throughout)
Felix: portable phone, copy of *Racing Post*
Simon: wrist-watch

SCENE 2

On stage: As before

Off stage: Small Union Jack (**Dave**)
Scripts (**Felix, Jo**)
Script (**Dave**)
Scripts (**Phyllida**)
Prompt script, revolve control box (**Jo**)

Personal: **Dave**: false beard

SCENE 3

On stage: As before

Off stage: Prompt script (used throughtout) (**Jo**)
              Script (used throughout) (**Felix**)
              Props basket on wheels containing sword, stuffed dog, old
                  lamp, box of practical torches, red and green "toadstool"
                  hats, saucepan with hole in bottom, mantle (**Dave**)

Personal: **Tom**: McDonald's burger
              Simon: scroll
              Dave: Groucho Marx moustache made of gaffa tape

SCENE 4

On stage: As before

Off stage: Trick flower (**Jo**)
              Aircraft batons (**Dave**)

Personal: **Dave**: paper bag

SCENE 5

On stage: As before

Off stage: Blanket (**Dave**)

Personal: **Jo**: head bandage

SCENE 6

On stage: As before

Off stage: Can of beer (**Puck: Jo**)
              2 small gossamer scarves (**Puck: Jo**)
              Giant green gossamer banner (**Simon**)
              Wood Nymph costume (**Dave**)
              Giant green gossamer banner (**Jo**)

Personal: **Felix**: wrist-watch, radio with headphones

ACT II
Scene 1

On stage: As before

Off stage: Pint of beer (**Tom**)
Script (**Simon**)
Puck costume (**Dave**)

Personal: **Demetrius (Tom)**: small breath freshener spray

Scene 2

On stage: As before

Off stage: Glittery blindfold (**Oberon: Felix**)
Paper flowers (**Fairies**)

Personal: **Lysander (Dave)**: blindfold
Demetrius (Tom): blindfold
Helena (Phyllida): blindfold
Hermia (Jo): blindfold

Scene 3

On stage: As before

Personal: **Mustardseed (Simon)**: confetti

Scene 4

On stage: As before

Off stage: Several large boards with words for audience (**2 Fairies**)
Cup of water (**Felix**)
Thisbe costume (**Stage Management**)

Personal: **Tom**: PE whistle

LIGHTING PLOT

Practical fittings required: lighted steps for Act II

ACT I

To open: House Lights to half

Cue 1	**Jo**: "Thank you."	(Page 1)
	House lights out, bring up full general lighting	

Cue 2	**Puck (Jo)** turns UR	(Page 50)
	Followspot UR	

Cue 4	**Dave** exits to the prompt corner	(Page 51)
	Cut general lighting, snap on worker lights	

ACT II

To open: Two spotlights play across tabs

Cue 5	As tabs rise	(Page 55)
	Cut spotlights, bring up full general lighting	

Cue 6	As **Felix** descends the steps	(Page 55)
	Snap on practicals in sequence	

Cue 7	**Felix** makes a grand gesture to the flies	(Page 56)
	Change to dim lighting	

Cue 8	**Jo**: "Lighting cue thirty-five — go!"	(Page 77)
	Increase lighting	

Cue 9	As **Jo** brings down the blindfold *Slowly dim lighting*	(Page 77)
Cue 10	**Bottom (Dave) as Pyramus** enters R *Fade to followspot on* **Dave**	(Page 97)
Cue 11	**Simon:** "Less light, less light!" *Black-out*	(Page 97)
Cue 12	**Jo:** "Torches off!" *Followspot on* **Dave**	(Page 98)
Cue 13	**Dave** congratulates the audience *Bring up full general lighting*	(Page 98)
Cue 14	**Simon** opens the portals *Fade to spot on* **Simon**	(Page 98)
Cue 15	**Simon** closes the portals *Black-out. When ready bring up full general lighting*	(Page 99)
Cue 16	**Phyllida:** "No." *Dim lighting; bring up soft spot on* **Jo**	(Page 100)

EFFECTS PLOT

ACT I

Cue 1 To open (Page 1)
Mendelssohn's "Dream" music; smoke

Cue 2 The **Fairies** dance (Page 1)
Clock strikes in the distance

Cue 3 To open SCENE 2 (Page 14)
As cue 1

Cue 4 **Tom** swiftly exits UR (Page 14)
Repeat cue 2

Cue 5 To cover scene change (Page 27)
Repeat cue 1; continue music, smoke to open Scene 4

Cue 6 **Phyllida** exits L (Page 34)
Maroon

Cue 7 **Jo** flies off L (Page 36)
Sound of breaking glass

Cue 8 To open SCENE 5 (Page 37)
Music

Cue 9 **Lysander (Dave)**: "... all his rest." (Page 38)
Ethereal music

Cue 10 To open SCENE 6 (Page 42)
Music

PRINTED IN GREAT BRITAIN BY
THE LONGDUNN PRESS LTD., BRISTOL.